THE WAR AGAINST THE NAZI U-BOATS 1942 – 1944

THE ANTISUBMARINE COMMAND

L. DOUGLAS KEENEY

PUBLISHED BY PREMIERE

CONTENTS

FOREWORD

The clouds of World War II were casting long and increasingly dark shadows across the face of America. By 1942, with the exception of neutral countries such as Spain, Switzerland and Sweden, the continent of Europe had been overrun by the Germans with just Britain and Russia holding them back from compete domination. On the other side of the world, Imperial Japan had a pincer-like grip on the remainder of the nations with occupation forces stretching from the Aleutians to New Guinea leaving just a narrow sea lane to Australia, which was also in jeopardy. If Japan were to prevail in the East and Germany in the West, North America would be an isolated continent surrounded by hostile nations on both sides.

Thus began the end. The Battle for the Atlantic pitted the Nazi wolf packs against the destroyer escorts of both navies, plus the RAF and, starting in 1942, the United States Army Air Force. But the tool that really did it was the B-24 Liberator. "The VLR [very long range] B-24 Liberator aircraft of RAF 120th Squadron was the weapon system which tipped the battle in favor of the Allies," wrote Chipman. "What made the aircraft such an effective weapon against the U-boat was their high speed relative to a surface vessel, a speed which permitted them to search a much greater area than a ship.

"In October 1942, the US Army Air Forces entered the Atlantic war by creating several land-based antisubmarine squadrons. Officially known as the US Army Air Forces' Antisubmarine Command, these units were designed to help the US Navy hunt for enemy submarines, which, at the time, were patrolling along the Atlantic coast and in the Caribbean.

"In November 1942, 21 American B-24s landed in South England and began flying out of St. Eval, Cornwall. Between December and March, they flew several patrols across the Bay of Biscay searching for and attacking various German submarines. On occasion they encountered German Junkers Ju-88 aircraft and had to fight their way back to England."

This remarkable restoration brings back to life the original 300-page report written by in 1945 by Arthur B. Ferguson, Assistant Chief of Air Staff, Intelligence, Historical Division of the United States Army Air Forces. Ferguson's fine history reminds us yet again of another crucial mission flown by the World War II airmen. For aviation and history buffs, and all those who enjoy an engaging story exceptionally well told, this is a wonderful addition to your library and the newest installment to our series of books under the banner of the Untold Stories of World War II..

1

THE BACKGROUND

In the days immediately following the attack on Pearl Harbor, the armed forces of the United States had to face the threat of a similar catastrophe on their eastern defenses. The Germans fully appreciated the advantages of swift offensive action in the Atlantic. They knew that American participation in the war would depend on the free and rapid movement of supply. Consequently, with the entry of the United States into active warfare, the Battle of the Atlantic became a key point in German strategy. And the Germans possessed in their submarine fleet, already used with devastating effect in the eastern Atlantic, the means of prosecuting this "trade war" to the utmost. It is not yet clear why the U-boats took nearly a month to become operative in American waters, but it appears that a detachment of the German submarine fleet was sent to the western Atlantic as soon as practicable after the formal entry of the United States into the war.

On 31 December a Coast Guard cutter reported a periscope in Portland Channel, and on 7 January an Army plane sighted a submarine off the coast of New Jersey. On that same day the Navy reported the presence of a fleet of U-boats in the waters south of Newfoundland. The SS Cyclope was sunk off Nova Scotia on 11 January; three days later the tanker Horness went down southeast of Montauk Point, Long Island. These sinking's merely head the tragically long list of similar losses which served almost more than the disaster of Pearl Harbor to bring home to the American public the grim realities of total war. Here was not only a drain on supply lines of our war effort, perilously thin at best, but an attack virtually on our Atlantic seaboard. In the remaining 17 days of January, 13 more ships sank in the North Atlantic Naval Coastal Frontier.

The situation rapidly became desperate. During the 76 days following the sinking of the Horness, 53 ships amounting to over 300,000 gross tons had gone down. With March sinking's at an annual rate of over 2,000,000 tons, the morale of merchant crews showed signs of rapid deterioration, and insurance companies had ceased writing marine insurance. Worst of all was the fact that, prior to May 1942, the enemy submarines operated with relative impunity in American coastal waters.

The question thus arose: what sort of antisubmarine defense could be brought to bear against this threat to the entire U.S. strategy in the Atlantic? According to general defense plans, which will be discussed in some detail a little later, the Navy had assumed responsibility for operations beyond the coast line, leaving to Army aircraft only a supporting, emergency role in coastal defense. Steps had been taken to provide the means of cooperation between the services, resulting in the completion of a joint control and information center at New York 4 days after war was declared. Nevertheless, the shock of Pearl Harbor found the Navy quite unable to carry on the offshore patrol necessary to the fulfillment of its mission. The Commander of the North Atlantic Naval Coastal Frontier (later, Eastern Sea Frontier), on whom fell naturally the initial responsibility for countering the submarine menace, had at his disposal on 7 December 1941 approximately 30 surface vessels, including 4 PY boats, 4 SC boats, one 165-foot Coast Guard cutter, six 125-foot Coast Guard cutters, 2 PG boats, and 3 Eagle boats to patrol the 1200-mille coast line from Maine to Key West. Of this force he wrote to COMINCH on 22 December: "There is not a single vessel available that an enemy submarine could not out-distance when operating on the surface. In most cases the guns of these vessels would be out-ranged by those of the submarine." Nor was it possible to augment the surface forces rapidly enough to make antisubmarine patrol, even convoy, practicable. The only destroyers available were those which happened to be in the ESF on fleet duties. In actual practice an average of only two destroyers per day was available for use. Repeated requests made to COMINCH for reinforcements apparently could not be met. For example, on 30 March 1942 the Commander, ESF sent a message in which he requested additional destroyers because four submarines had been sighted off Cape Hatteras and two more were believed to be operating there, while all except one of the four destroyers in the area were searching for survivors of a lost ship or were refueling or were under repair. COMINCH replied on 31 March briefly: "Your knowledge of other demands for DD's as imperative as your own is not given sufficient credit in your message 302318."

If the surface forces were wholly inadequate, the naval air arm was little stronger. In December, the naval planes at the disposal of the Commander, ESF totaled 103. Of these, however, the majority were trainers or utility ships; only one was listed as a bomber, although 9 were classified as patrol or torpedo bombers. A month later the picture appeared little if at all brighter. Of the 63 aircraft available for duty between Salem and Elizabeth City (including four lighter-than-air ships at Lakehurst), only 49 were actually in commission. Of these, the majority could carry only one depth bomb. Adm. Adolphus Andrews, Commander, ESF summed up the air situation in words reminiscent of those he used to describe the paucity of surface vessels. He wrote to COMINCH on 14 January 1942: "There are no effective planes attached to the frontier, First, Third, Fourth, or Fifth Naval District capable of maintaining long-range seaward patrols." Nor did he receive much more comfort from higher headquarters on this topic than on that of the extra destroyers. In reply to his urgent request for air reinforcement he received the reply that allocation of additional air forces was "dependent on future production." Here, as elsewhere in the early days of 1942, the demands for men and equipment were great but the supply small.

So the burden for antisubmarine patrol fell mainly on the Army Air Forces whose units had been neither trained nor equipped for that specific task, but were nevertheless better able than the Navy's air arm to present a menacing front to the enemy. As soon as the news of Pearl Harbor arrived, the Commander of the North Atlantic Naval coastal Frontier requested the Commanding General of the Eastern Defense Command to undertake offshore patrols with all available aircraft. On the afternoon of 8 December

1941, units of the I Bomber Command began overwater patrols, and for nearly 10 months that command bore the brunt of the air war against the U-boats. But it was a motley array of aircraft that the Bomber Command assembled in December and January to meet the submarine threat. Almost on the same day on which it was called upon to undertake overwater patrol duties was stripped of the best trained of its tactical units for missions on the West Coast and for overseas assignment. Every available Army plane in the First Air Force capable of carrying a bomb load was drafted to augment what was left of I Bomber Command. As a result of these frantic efforts approximately 10 two-engine aircraft of various sizes and types were assembled and placed at the disposal of the naval commander. To this force, likened by one observer to the taxi cab army by means of which the French attempted, in 1914, to stem the German advance, the I Air Support Command added substantial aid in the way of reconnaissance. Admiral Andrews described the operation of these Army air units, on 14 January 1942, as follows:

The Army Air Support Command is operating during daylight hours patrols in single-motored land observation planes extending about forty miles offshore from Portland, Maine, to Wilmington, NC. These planes are not armed and carry only sufficient fuel for flights of between two or three hours. The pilots are inexperienced in the type of work they are endeavoring to do. Not more than ten of these observation planes are in the air along the Coastal Frontier at any one time.

The First Bomber Command has been maintaining, since the week of 7 December 1941, patrols from Westover Field, Mass.; Mitchell Field, NY; and Langley field, VA; and as of 11 January 1942 are commencing patrols from Bangor, Maine. These patrols, averaging three planes each, have extended, weather permitting and according to the type of plane, to a maximum distance of six hundred miles to sea. Two flights each day are being made from the aforementioned fields. The First Bomber Command has been utilizing approximately half of its available equipment in order to maintain these patrols, at the expense of a striking force which could be called upon in case of enemy attack.

It was a creditable effort, all things considered, but the Army forces were themselves pitifully inadequate. By 31 January 1943, the I Air Support Command reported 114 planes, of which 93 were in commission; the I Bomber Command numbered 119 planes of which only 45 were carried as in commission.

If the forces available during December and January for anti-submarine activity were too small for the job, they were even weaker in equipment and organization. Hunting submarines is a highly specialized business, as all those concerned found out during the next few months. Yet little had been done prior to the outbreak of hostilities to develop the specialized technique and materials required to carry it on successfully. Except for the establishment of a Joint Control and Information Center little had been done to set up the system of communication and intelligence necessary to cope adequately with such a highly mobile, not to say illusive, enemy. Fortunately, the U-boats did not begin operations in US waters for nearly a month, which gave the I Bomber Command time to organize some sort of wire communication to all its bases, to establish an intelligence system through which information could be relayed from Bomber Command headquarters to the squadron operations room, and from Bomber Command airplanes to headquarters. By the end of January, however, the problem of transmitting intelligence remained a vexing one.

The Army suffered also from poorly equipped planes and inadequately trained personnel. Charges to this effect were frequently made and were well justified. Most of the units involved in the anti-submarine war were, at this early date, still in a training status, and those best trained had been taken away for service in the West. In addition, prowar agreements had assigned overwater operations to the Navy and had placed restrictions on Army overwater flying. So it is scarcely surprising that the Army planes entered on their adopted task with demolition bombs instead of depth charges and with crews who were ill-trained in naval identification or in the best method of attacking submarines. The aircraft used against the U-boats were generally unsuited to that kind of work. All, with the exception of a squadron of B-17's, were of relatively short range and limited carrying capacity. And all, of course, as yet lacked special detection equipment. The old B-18, though obsolescent, proved to be the most useful in the early months, but even they were at first scarce.

Those in charge of the antisubmarine war attacked these problems wholeheartedly. They revived the training program to convert crews, hitherto accustomed only to high-altitude bombings, to the intricacies of low-level attack on submerged targets. They adapted the aircraft as fast as the materials became available and the necessary research could bear fruit. As operations continued and experience was collected, it became evident that successful warfare against U-boats demanded improved methods of joint control in order to dispatch both air and surface forces to the scene of a sighting as rapidly as the situation required. Here the British, who had accumulated a good deal of experience in this sort of work, contributed vitally to the improvement of the joint control system. With the help of several experienced liaison officers, sent to America for the purpose, a new "control room" was projected which led to more effective cooperation between Army and Navy forces. The original control room permitted "joint" operations, but the two services worked independently in different parts of the same building, each maintaining its own situation plot and receiving intelligence from different sources. There was little interchange of information or methods.

By the end of March it is possible to notice very real improvement in the situation. Though the U-boats continued in increasing numbers to exact an increasing toll of merchant shipping, they also met increasing opposition in the coastal waters. Operational hours flown by AAF planes in March were well over double those flown in January. Relatively few attacks were made even yet, and their quality left much to be desired. But the submarines were being forced more and more to submerge, which prevented as free hunting on their part as they had formerly enjoyed. A very few Army planes were beginning to be equipped with radar, another stop, though a small one, in the right direction. In March, too, the first offshore patrol missions were flown by the Civil Air Patrol. Although totally insu8ited in both training and equipment to antisubmarine warfare, these auxiliary units were able to assume some of the burden of reconnaissance flying.

Many difficulties of course remained. More and better-trained personnel, more and better-equipped aircraft, a better communications system—these were only the more obvious requirements in the Army antisubmarine force. Much more deeply rooted was the problem of jurisdiction which arose out of the anomalous position of the AAF units engaged in antisubmarine operations. The I Bomber Command was, in fact, waging full-scale antisubmarine war, yet it enjoyed no correspondingly adequate legal position. It was still theoretically acting in an emergency capacity, in support of Naval forces, and might at any time be withdrawn to its normal duties of bombardment. Indeed, training had to be conducted literally on two levels both for low-level antisubmarine attacks and for high-level bombing in connection with coastal defense. Worse still, no system of unified command had been set up specifically for that type of joint operations peculiar to antisubmarine warfare. Prior to 26 March 1942, in fact, even the command relationship existing between Bomber Command and the Eastern Sea Frontier remained indefinite, the former serving without specific directives under the "operational control" of the latter. Any decision on these questions of jurisdiction would necessarily have involved a radical review of the existing relationship between the services, especially in their relation to the air arm. And some decision was obviously necessary if antisubmarine operations were not to founder hopelessly in a maze of overlapping jurisdictional boundaries and tortuous command channels. It was a kind of fighting that demanded extreme mobility on the part of the antisubmarine forces and almost instantaneous transmission of intelligence if the enemy, itself extremely mobile and under closely integrated command, were to be successfully engaged.

Almost from the beginning it began to appear that, if the Army Air Forces were to continue in the antisubmarine business, their units engaged in that work would have to be organized into a specially trained and equipped command with antisubmarine operations as its sole duty. Such a prospect at once raised a family of problems. In the first place, who, Army or Navy, should control this command? Secondly, should it be deployed defensively, in support of the fleet, primarily for the protection of the shipping lanes, or as a highly mobile force capable of carrying the battle aggressively to the enemy wherever the latter might be located? On these two grounds, the jurisdictional and the strategic, there arose a long and intensive controversy, a debate which centered on the creation, organization, and deployment of an AAF antisubmarine command, but which involved issues of much broader scope. In order, therefore, to understand these issues and to explain the confusion as a result of which the Army Air Forces found itself engaged in the submarine hunt, it will be necessary to review in some detail the evolution of policy governing the use of the air arm in overwater operations.

Ever since the advent of air power the Army and the Navy had argued over its control. Each service took a logical enough position. To the Army, control of land-based aircraft whether operating over land or water should be its responsibility. To the Navy, it seemed equally natural that operations over water, against seaborne targets, should be a naval responsibility. It all depended on where the respective arguments started: if it was a question of the primary mission of land-based aircraft, as a result of which they had been developed as such, the Army had a strong position; if it became a question of where the actual operations took place, whether as a result of the primary mission of the forces or merely ancillary to it, the Navy was well able to claim control over seaward aviation. No one disputed the Navy's control over seaplanes and carrier-based aircraft which operated clearly as an arm of the fleet. Actually, logic had very little to do with the problem. Since the air was a medium which extended over both land and water, arguments concerning its control could drift more or loss at will. So it all became a question which would have to be answered either arbitrarily, by some competent authority, or with reference to some factors contingent upon the tactical or strategic situation. As things turned out, it was answered by both.

As early as 1920 it had been recognized that, in providing an air arm for both services, there lay a serious danger of duplicating installations and equipment. In that year Congress had enacted that Army aviation should control all aerial operations from land bases and that naval aviation should control all such activity attached to the Fleet; including the maintenance of such shore installations as were necessary for operation, experimentation, and training connected with the Fleet.

Joint Action of the Army and Navy, 1935 (ETP-155) did much to clarify the relationship between the services. The Navy not only retained control of aviation connected with the Fleet, but was given responsibility for all inshore and offshore patrol for the purpose of protecting shipping and defending the coastal frontier. It was further stated that Army aircraft might temporarily execute Navy functions in support of, or in lieu of, Navy forces, and conversely, that Navy aircraft might be called upon to support land operations. In neither case should any restriction be placed by one service on the freedom of the other to use its power against the enemy should the need arise. Each service was declared responsible for providing the aircraft needed for the proper performance of its primary function: in the Army's case, the conduct of air operations over land and such air operations over the sea as were incident to the accomplishment of Army functions; in the case of the Navy, conduct of operations over the sea and such air operations over the land as were incident to the accomplishment of Navy functions.

All of which left the responsibility for the conduct of seaward patrols and the protection of shipping pretty definitely up to the Navy. But no formal agreement could be expected to end discussion on the matter, especially since the particular tactical situation was likely to change frequently. It was still, for example, an open question whether the Navy should control all air operations in frontier defense or whether it should control only those operations specifically in support of the Fleet. Naval spokesmen claimed that unity of command should be vested in whichever service held paramount importance in a given situation. Then, assuming that naval preeminence existed over land and air forces in all coastal defense, they claimed that unity of command in such operations should rest with the Navy. The Army, sensing a train of logic which might prove ruinous to its control of air forces, raised its voice in protest. The assumption of naval preeminence in coastal defense it declared unsound, witness the case of Alaska where land-based bombers were likely to be the principal arm employed. Furthermore, since most situations in which the Navy would be called upon for defensive operations would be ones in which the air forces would also be present, owing to their mobility and striking power, the Navy would, according to this argument, gain control of Army air forces, wherever the latter were most likely to be used in a tactical situation. This, the Army felt, would lead ultimately to complete naval control of the Army air forces. In short, the Army felt that the primary mission of its air arm was not support of the Navy, however likely such support might be in frontier defense.

When it came time to implement plans for frontier defense, it was clear that the Navy held the responsibility for protection of coastwise shipping and for the conduct of offshore patrols. And this province was guarded jealously. Units of the GHQ Air Force had been effectively discouraged from undertaking practice reconnaissance flights over water beyond the 100-mile limit, and their part in joint Army-Navy exercises had been strictly limited to a supporting role against a carrier-borne or shore attack; this despite the fact that plans explicitly made the GHQ Air Force responsible for whatever reconnaissance was essential to its combat efficiency in operations along the coast, regardless of whether or not the Fleet were present. Without an air arm trained in long- or even medium-range reconnaissance over water, the seaboard would clearly become vulnerable to submarine attack. Yet the Navy had done very little to prepare for antisubmarine air patrol by any type of aircraft, much less by long-range types. Joint Action had not only implied that this function belonged to the Navy, but had stated that it was up to the Navy to provide and maintain the equipment and installations necessary to the fulfillment of that function. Yet 7 December 1941 found the North Atlantic Naval Coastal Frontier practically without effective planes capable of conducting long-range seaward patrols, and with pathetically few surface craft capable of chasing a submarine.

Fortunately, some preparations had been made for joint operations. A "joint" control room had almost been completed and provision had been made for I Bomber Command and I Air Support Command to operate on seaward patrol missions wherever requested to do so by the naval authority. It was in fulfillment of these plans that the I Bomber Command undertook seaward patrol duty promptly on 8 December. But even this meager air force had been equipped not for antisubmarine activity but for normal bombardment action, and had been systematically discouraged from increasing its knowledge of overwater flying.

Every contingency, including enemy submarine activity in the coastal shipping lanes, had been considered in Joint Action. Yet nothing had been planned specifically to counter a campaign by enemy submarine forces. Training exercises off the Atlantic coast had apparently envisaged a surface task force, supported by carrier-based aircraft, as the only likely form of enemy action. The British had also failed at first to take the U-boat threat seriously, feeling that it should not be relatively as great in this as in the last war. After the Germans had built submarine bases on the west coast of

Franco, however, the British answered this increased menace by creating the Coastal Command, a separate RAF agency under the operational control of the Admiralty. No such plan had been laid or agencies established in the United States.

By the time the German submarines began to appear in American waters, the idea had become pretty well fixed that long- and medium-range land-based bombers would be, if not the backbone of the antisubmarine campaign, at least in indispensible part of its composition, especially in view of the fact that operations from ice-bound north Atlantic bases would be limited virtually to aircraft of that type. In a very natural effort to implement the Navy's responsibility for offshore patrol, Admiral King at once requested that 200 B-24's and 400 B-25's be allocated from future production of Army-type planes for Navy use, the total number to be made available by 1 July 1943. This request did little to improve relations between the services, coming as it did on top of a long discussion of the problem of jurisdiction over coastal defense operations, and at a time when the Army was confronted by urgent obligations in half a dozen theaters, all demanding heavy-and medium-bombardment planes. The Navy received part, though not all, of the Army-type allocations asked for, but had to be content for the time being with the forces supplied mainly by the I Bomber Command and related units. Considerable effort was made to increase the number of aircraft allocated by the Army to antisubmarine activity, but it was felt in the War Department that diversion beyond that already made would seriously jeopardize other equally important projects.

And so, from the very first, the Army's participation in the antisubmarine campaign became involved in, and at times overshadowed by, the issues of jurisdiction and organization which it had raised. The Navy request for Army-type planes raised again, or rather reinvigorated, the standing controversy concerning control of the air arm. To Admiral King's request, General Arnold replied that for the Navy to build up a force of land-based aircraft would lead to a duplication of equipment, maintenance, and supply that would eventually "deny the essential differences between armies and navies." Some felt that, if Army aircraft were so vital a part of coastal defense, unity of command over joint operations in the coastal frontiers should be vested in the Army. This notion, of course, ran counter to the established policy as outlined in Joint Action, and would in any cases have lacked the support of the Navy. General Arnold proposed to settle the question in a practical compromise. In a letter to Admiral King, 9 May 1942, he wrote: "to meet the present situation, I propose to recommend the establishment of a Coastal Command, within the Army Air Corps which will have for its purpose operations similar to the Coastal Command, RAF," operating "when necessary under the control of the proper Naval authority." The virtues of such an organization would, he felt, be many: it would not only do the job, it would also have the flexibility necessary for antisubmarine action, and could readily be decreased as the need decreased, the units then simply reverting to normal bombardment duty without becoming stranded wastefully in a naval program which left no place for them. In this proposal General Arnold pointed the way to the settlement finally adopted in the creation of the AAF Antisubmarine Command.

Many other influences were tending in the same direction by May of 1942. Above all, of course, was the ugly fact that in that month sinking's in the sea frontiers had risen to a new and terrifying point. Something had obviously to be done to improve the organization of the antisubmarine campaign. Closely related was the fact that the enemy had shifted his strategy and had once more caught the US defenses badly prepared. Most of the May sinking's had occurred in the Gulf and Caribbean areas. Scarcely adequate to protect shipping in the ESP, the existing organization of antisubmarine operations proved quite inadequate to cope with a greatly extended area of activity.

In answer to a request for reinforcement from the Commander, Gulf Sea Frontier, a few B-18's were sent south, and shortly after, on 26 May, Maj. Gen. Follett Bradley, Commanding General of the First Air Force, created the Gulf Task Force. This unit was to control all aircraft of the First Air Force which were operating, according to the agreement of the Joint Chiefs of Staff for such situations, under the operational control of the Gulf Sea Frontier. For a time located at Charleston, SC, the new headquarters was finally set up at Miami.

The situation in the Gulf and Caribbean areas had, however, become so serious that General Arnold requested the Third Air Force to use certain of its units for antisubmarine patrol during their regular overwater training missions. General Frank responded by advising the placing of the appropriate units under the operational control of the Gulf Task Force and the routing of training missions over sea and Gulf shipping lanes. This plan was approved on 1 July, and steps were at once taken to put it into effect. Meanwhile, arrangements were made to establish a combined operations center at Miami, to be built on the general pattern being laid down for similar purposes in New York City. This project was initiated early in June.

Considerable progress was made in relocating units to meet the expanded and fluid nature of the campaign. Beginning in January with operations from four states only, from Bangor, Maine, to Langley Field, VA, the I Bomber Command by September 1942 was operating in seven states, from Westover Field, Mass, to Galveston, TX.

Despite this energetic effort to meet a rapidly changing situation with complicated machinery constructed essentially on static principles, the extension of AAP antisubmarine operations emphasized the need for reform in the existing system of joint command. Only recently had any attempt been made to clarify even this existing system. Prior to 26 March 1942, units of the I Bomber Command and the I Air Support Command had been operating under the control of the Commander, Eastern Sea Frontier, but the system rested only on very general definitions set forth in Joint Action. And there had been some talk of "mutual cooperation" rather than "unity of command." On that date the Joint Chiefs of Staff sent a message to the commanding generals of the defense commands which read, in extract, as follows:

```
Pending the reaching of agreements as to terms under which unity of
command will be exercised … unity of command as set forth in … Joint
Action of the Army and Navy, 1935, is hereby vested in sea Frontier
Commands over all Navy forces duly allocated thereto and over all Army air
units allocated by defense commanders over the sea for the protection of
shipping and for antisubmarine and other operations … Defense commanders
will allocate Army air units on full time basis but may rotate them in not
less then two week periods as requisite for essential training …
```

This seemed a convenient temporary arrangement, but in reality it did nothing to meet the administrative and tactical problems. It merely made more definite what had hitherto been left studiously vague.

The fact was that the two services were not organized for this type of joint control. Command boundaries overlapped: the areas assigned to the First Air Force and the I Bomber Command extended beyond the Eastern Sea Frontier into the territory of the Gulf Sea Frontier, and the Third Air Force had to share the operational control of the Commander, Gulf Sea Frontier with the First Air Force. Worse than that, joint operations involved two complete sets of headquarters through which orders must be filtered before reaching the combat unit.

General McNarney described the command situation in April as follows:

```
At present the Bomber Command is allocated to the Eastern Sea Frontier
for operational control. The Civil Air Patrol is under the Air Support
Command for operational control. The Air Support Command is under the
Bomber Command for operational control. The Bomber Command is operating
under a directive from the Navy, which was a two page, seven paragraph
letter, which was very verbose.
```

He might have added that the Bomber Command was under the First Air Force and the Eastern Defense Command for administration, if any further complication were desired.

Desired or not, further complication did enter the picture when in May it became necessary to extend operations into the Gulf and Caribbean areas. The I Bomber Command was still the only agency equipped and situated to provide the Army air coverage necessary for successful antisubmarine activity. It was therefore essential to extend its operation southward to include the entire EDO and that part of the Southern Defense Command which borders on the Gulf of Mexico. In this area I Bomber Command operated under the control of the Gulf Sea Frontier. To augment this over-extended force, some aircraft had been loaned by the Third Air Force to the EST and GSF commanders for patrol purposes. These units, however, operated under the direct control of the Bomber Command, which retained responsibility for Army antisubmarine patrol in the coastal frontiers. The plight of these few pilots, who were connected administratively or operationally with two defense commands, two sea frontiers, two air forces, and an antisubmarine bomber command, simply represents the reduction ad absurdum of the command situation.

The trouble was obvious. A multiplicity of headquarters would have slowed up the functioning of any dependent organization. It was all the more serious in its effects on antisubmarine operations which depended above all else on rapid coordination and extreme nobility. The division of the sea frontiers into districts and subdistricts had been enough of a handicap especially in view of the habit of thinking in terms of rigid boundaries or "chop lines" which seemed to be an ingrained part of the naval administrative mind. Yet local arrangement had been made to mitigate this handicap. Army air units were apparently not attached to district naval commanders, a practice which, if adopted, would have ruined the effectiveness of the Army antisubmarine forces. The real trouble came when aircraft were required in other sea frontiers, all of which were under COMMINCH, but without liaison or means of rapid inter-communication. Yet the antisubmarine campaign depended on the ability of air striking units to fellow the submarines wherever they might go and to change stations rapidly.

Unity of command, then, became the first prerequisite for improved operations. The antisubmarine campaign needed other things: better equipment, a better training program, a better communication system, and an organization devoted completely to the task of hunting U-boats, unimpeded by competing claims on its services. Above all, it required mobility of forces. But all these needs were subordinate to, and in one way or another dependent upon, the attaining of unity of command.

With these needs in mind, and impelled by the desperate shipping situation, the War Department began, in May, to take concerted action to improve the situation. On the 20th of that month, Maj. Gen. Dwight D. Eisenhower, then Assistant Chief of Staff, OPD, directed the commanding generals of the AAF and the EDS to do everything in their power to improve the antisubmarine activity being undertaken by the First Air Force. Specifically he directed that all available planes on the eastern seaboard be fitted with bomb racks and all B-18 air craft be equipped with radar, even at the expense of prior allocations. All necessary bases were to be made available, and the EDC was to cooperate with the First Air Force in the solution of problems of supply, maintenance, and communications for the antisubmarine squadrons. An organization was to be established "with the least possible delay" for the purpose of engaging in the development of antisubmarine weapons, tactics, and techniques in cooperation with all agencies working toward a similar end. A training unit was also authorized in order to make available crews trained in the use of these devices and techniques.

Finally, General Arnold was requested to reorganize the I Bomber Command in such a way as to "fulfill the special requirements of antisubmarine and allied air operations, in consonance with the Army responsibility in operating in support of, or in lieu of naval forces for protection of shipping."

This action on the part of the War Department General Staff marks the beginning of plans for a separate, mobile air striking force, organized within the Army for the sole purpose of hunting submarines. In taking this action the Army in effect accepted the responsibility for a job not generally considered part of its function. No longer considered simply as an emergency, short-term measure, the participation of AAF units in the antisubmarine war now became admittedly part of the Army program. And, in the circumstances, the Army found itself in a relatively strong position. Its air force had the weapons, and had already taken part in antisubmarine activity for nearly 5 months during which time it had developed some sort of organization, some special techniques, and many ambitious plans.

Plans of a more or less specific nature soon followed. General Eisenhower had stated in his directive that "although unity of command is vested in the Navy, it is felt that the Army must be prepared to submit recommendations and to take every action to make antisubmarine warfare fully effective." He had requested that General Bradley and Brig. Gen. Westside T. Larson, Commanding General, I Bomber Command, confer with the Assistant Chief of Staff and present plans for future development.

Plans had for some weeks been evolving in the minds of the AAF officials concerned. In general they had been shaped along the lines suggested in General Eisenhower's directive: a separate organization was to be created for the purpose of waging antisubmarine warfare, with mobility and striking power as its chief characteristic, and with an experimental agency acting as an auxiliary for developing new techniques and for training personnel in their use. But they were naturally more specific and somewhat more radical in their color than that directive called for. Through all this initial planning can be seen the strong influence of the British Coastal Command. And naturally so, because that command had pioneered since the beginning of the war in antisubmarine warfare under circumstances roughly analogous to those in which the American forces found themselves in 1942. A few officers from the British Coastal Command had been detailed to advise the I Bomber Command in its early efforts to combat the U-boats, and their influence was in many respects decisive. In February, Wing Commander P.F. Canning, RAF, had outlined the Coastal Command system of operational control as a pattern for a similar organization modified to suit the situation in the western Atlantic. Admittedly far from perfect, this system bore the authority of 4 years' experience in joint action for the specific purpose of antisubmarine warfare. In March, Wing Commander S.R. Libles, RAF, submitted a report on his observations of antisubmarine activity in which he stressed the need for a clearer allocation of responsibility between Army and Navy, for closer cooperation between the headquarters involved, and for a decreased emphasis on rigid command boundaries. All these factors pointed toward the ultimate solution in the form of a separate command, presumably shaped on lines similar to those of the British Coastal Command.

General Eisenhower had suggested that a conference on antisubmarine measures be held in Washington. In preparation for this meeting, Generals Bradley and Larson drew up and discussed various plans. Although a detailed critique of these proposals is unnecessary, some of the points highlighted in them clarify the train of thought that led to the establishment of the Antisubmarine Command. A précis of the principal plans follows:

1. The basic principle upon which successful antisubmarine warfare must rest is unity of command. The submarine possesses great mobility; successful action against it necessitates elimination of overlapping jurisdiction in order that prompt action may be facilitated. Command channels must be direct, and the "maddening and intolerable" system of verbal orders from one office and written orders from another must be eliminated. Mobility is essential. A successful antisubmarine force must be able to move units from point to point to meet the requirements of a shifting strategic situation.

2. A "Coastal Air Force" should be organized with the I Bomber Command as its nucleus. The chain of command then would be from Commanding General, AAF, the Commanding General, Coastal Air Force,

to Coastal Air Force Controller to Squadron Commander. An operations control room would be set up at each base, and steps would be taken to establish adequate coordination of intelligence with the Navy. The Navy would, however, no longer exercise direct operational control over Army planes, because all orders would pass through Headquarters, Coastal Air Force.

3. In the Coastal Air Force, the area of operation would be unlimited and not confined by existing boundaries of commands having other missions to perform.

4. A chain of bases should be set up on the Atlantic coast to operate directly under the Coastal Air Force. Weather, intelligence, communications, maintenance and housing and all housekeeping facilities would be provided by the bases, leaving the striking forces to consist of combat and key personnel only. The combat squadrons would therefore be "in reality mobile."

Another plan, evidently prepared by General Bradley for use in the conference with General Eisenhower, proposed that the I Bomber Command, or similar organization, be charged with the protection of all coastal shipping, the operation to be under the direct control of the Commanding General of the First Air Force. Not only would all Army aircraft thus be placed under an Army officer, but all Navy and Marine heavier-than-air aircraft allocated to antisubmarine activity would also be under the I Bomber Command for operational control, only dirigibles (a waning force) remaining under the Navy.

All other coordination's between Army and Navy to be by cooperation rather than by unity of command, as is now the case between Eastern Defense Command and Eastern Sea Frontier. If operational control by Navy must be continued, a single Navy commander, not three, should be responsible for the entire East and Gulf Coasts and Bermuda, and exercise operational control or unity of command over those Army Air Forcer which are allotted to him.

In short, the Navy had been relegated to a position of remote and shadowy authority. But they left no doubt on certain other points: the need for unity of command, a more direct chain of command, greater potential mobility, and a continued and increased participation of Army air forces in the "trade war," all of which depended in some way on the creation of a separate command, organized, trained, and equipped for the purpose.

Running through this entire discussion there may be discerned an already well defined strategic doctrine, namely, that, in antisubmarine warfare, defensive measures, though essential, can never destroy the U-boat menace, but must be sup0plemented by a vigorous offensive campaign. The authors of the plans outlined above considered the protection of convoys by aircraft "a last ditch defense." Such purely defensive tactics were, and should be, the first priority, but they were "the smaller part of the total effort necessary to force the enemy from our coastal waters." A well-coordinated offensive by aircraft and surface vessels could drive the enemy craft a considerable distance from the coast or restrict their operations to such an extent that their results would become negligible. Admittedly the airplane as it was then equipped failed to possess the necessary killing power to destroy the U-boat; but it did have great searching power, and was quite able to keep a submarine submerged so long that its effectiveness decreased. Whenever a sinking occurred or the presence of a submarine was detected, long-range planes should be sent to that area for intensive search. Constant patrol should be conducted within 300 miles of the coastline. Even if these measures failed to sink a single submarine, it was argued, they would keep the enemy submerged and so require him to use so much time going to and from his bases that his operating period would materially be shortened, Moreover, the submarines could thus be prevented from concentrating rapidly and effectively on convoys, and the morale of their crews would be seriously impaired.

Here again the example of the RAF Coastal Command exercised a profound influence. Although it had apparently taken the Admiralty some time to revise its doctrines to such an extent that it could incorporate within them an air striking force organized for an aggressive antisubmarine campaign, still that was the end finally attained. Two of the cardinal principles governing the British antisubmarine warfare were stated by Air Marshal Joubert: first, close cooperation between sea and air forces, between Admiralty and Coastal Command; and secondly, constant offensive action. He advised that:

While a certain amount of close escort of convoys, particularly when
threatened, is a necessary feature of air operations, the main method of
defeating the U-boat is to seek and strike. The greater portion of the
air available should always be engaged in the direct attack of U-boats
and the smallest possible number in direct protection of shipping. Our
experience is that a purely defensive policy only leads to heavy loss in
merchant shipping.

Ideas such as these may seem natural enough to those unacquainted with
the conflict of policies between Army and Navy. There would, for instance,
seem to be little objection on any score to action which, while preserving
the existing convoy system and routine patrol, would carry the war to the
enemy as well. But to organize an offensive would mean to reorganize the
entire antisubmarine campaign. Specifically it would require the creation of
just such a semi-independent and mobile command as the AAF planners
had in mind. For, at the time, only such a body could carry out a strategic
policy that reached beyond the Navy's defensive doctrine of convoy and offshore patrol, and be able to attack the U-boats at their point of greatest concentration. Moreover, the long-range Army-type bombers alone combined
the range and striking power necessary for such offensive action, and as yet
the AAF was better able than the Navy to equip such a force. In short, under
existing conditions, an offensive strategy simply would not fit into the Navy
scheme of things. Not only did it run counter to the Navy's preference for a
defensive antisubmarine war, but it also would tend to weaken naval control
over the Army elements engaged in the antisubmarine campaign.

By the summer of 1942, therefore, it is possible to see the outlines of
those two related controversies, the jurisdictional and the strategic, which
determined the history of the AAF antisubmarine effort. The AAF plane, as
shaped in May, could lead only in one direction. Unchecked they would
eventually have placed the entire responsibility for the air antisubmarine
campaign in the hands of those who held the aggressive strategic doctrine
and who were in immediate possession of the organization and the weapons
necessary to carry out that doctrine. But the Army plans did not remain
unchecked. They met the consistent opposition of the Navy, energetic in
this defensive action as in its defensive Battle of the Atlantic.

In view of all this discussion it is surprising to find formal action taking a
much slower and more compromising course. For the rest of the summer

little was done in a radical way to reorganize the antisubmarine campaign. In immediate response to General Eisenhower's directive of 20 May, General McNarnoy, Assistant Chief of Staff, WDGS, informed Admiral King that 10 B-18's, ASV-equipped, together with 10 additional medium bombers without ASV, had been sent to the bedeviled Gulf area where they would work under the operational control of the Gulf Sea Frontier commander. He also outlined a proposed reorganization of the Army antisubmarine program. The I Bomber Command was to be organized as a unit to wage antisubmarine "and related operations" on the East and Gulf coasts. Air bases were to be established at strategic locations in order to take maximum advantage of the mobility of land-based aircraft. As soon as available, ASV-equipped aircraft would be welded into units "particularly suited for hunting down and destroying enemy submarines by methods developed by our experimental units which have been operating off Cape Hatteras." Mobility was to be the keynote of this reorganized force. When a unit moved to an area outside the HDC, it would operate under the control of the particular sea frontier commander concerned, but it would still remain assigned to the I Bomber Command. "Movement to and operation in areas beyond the jurisdiction of the latter will be viewed as a temporary detachment therefrom."

Admiral King's reaction to these cautious proposals was expressed with equal caution. They were, he felt, satisfactory but he planned to place the control of aircraft assigned to each sea frontier in the hands of the commander of that frontier. Moreover, in providing air coverage for convoys it would not be necessary for planes attached to one frontier to operate in another "unless exceptional conditions make it necessary." In a note to the sea frontier commanders, concerning General McNarney's letter, he said, further: "It will be noted that the division of aircraft, both Army and Navy, as between the sea frontiers, will be a matter under the cognizance of the Commander in Chief, and that the air operations within the sea frontiers will be under the direction of the Commander Sea Frontier concerned." In other words, rigid geographic lines were to be retained in the use of Army planes, and such use was to be dictated unequivocally by naval authorities.

While these plans were under discussion, the heavy shipping losses continued at such an alarming rate that on 19 June 1942 General Marshall expressed to Admiral King his fear that "another month or two" of similar losses would "so cripple our means of transport that we will be unable to bring sufficient men and planes against the enemy in critical theaters to exercise a determining influence on the war." This note of alarm elicited a definite statement of the Navy's strategic doctrine in its campaign against the U-boat. Admiral King had already made it clear that the system of Navy regional control would remain a part of the united command that the Navy was to exercise. Now he set himself clearly in opposition to the Army's offensive doctrine. If that doctrine had not been emphasized officially, it had certainly been given enough informal currency to have established it as a basic point of difference between the services. And Admiral King apparently took General Marshall's memo as an implied criticism of the Navy's antisubmarine strategy. The Navy had, he said in reply, employed, and would continue to employ, all available forces in the antisubmarine war and that "not only the Navy itself but also all other agencies concerned must continue to intensify the antisubmarine effort." But that intensified effort to him meant intensified convey protection. "Escort," he declared, "is not just One way of handling the submarine menace; it is the only way that gives any promise of success ... We must get every ship that sails the seas under constant close protection." The work of the I "Bomber Command had been valuable in this respect, and after 15 May the coastal waters of the United States had been quite safe for coastwise shipping under convoy. The convoy system was being extended, as rapidly as possible, but the Army should supply at least 500 medium bombers for use in the four sea frontiers – Eastern, Gulf, Caribbean, and Panama – to augment the force of 850 planes the Navy hoped to operate in those areas.

The Army was thus exhorted to bend every effort in the common cause. It had, however, been far from idle. The I Bomber Command had been useful, if not determinative, in making the Atlantic seaboard unhealthy for U-boats. Lack of proper equipment and training continued to keep the quality of attacks on a comparatively low level. But, from July on, improvement in material and a half year of experience in actual submarine hunting had made it possible for the Army antisubmarine units to contribute

impressively to the campaign which made the Germans reconsider the value
of operations in US coastal waters

The figures themselves are misleading. In 59,243 operational hours
flown between January and October 1942, not many more than 200 sightings were reported, of which several were no doubt mistaken identification
by inexperienced crews. In 81 instances attacks followed which resulted in
one U-boat definitely destroyed, six seriously damaged, and seven damaged
to some extent. The aircraft made their contribution rather in forcing submarines to submerge so frequently that their targets were lost and their
activity slowed up to the point where the returns became marginal or sub-
marginal.

The quality of the patrols and especially of the attacks improved steadily
as suitable equipment became available and crews gained in experience. The
first attack that was assessed as in any degree damaging in the U-boat did
not occur until 2 April 1942. During the nest 4 months the bulk of the damaging attacks were made. The frequency of attacks roughly paralleled the
density of U-boats in the area and also the sinking of merchant vessels. It is
estimated that, during May and June, when the U-boats were thickest and
their work most deadly, each was attacked on an average of twice each
month by aircraft of the I Bomber Command.

After June, enemy activity fell off rapidly in the coastal waters. Her again
a look at the figures alone would convey a false impression. It is clear from
them, and perfectly true, that in August the enemy began to withdraw to
other areas, and by October had virtually abandoned the Eastern and Gulf
Sea Frontiers. After 4 September no more bombings occurred in 1942 as a
result of enemy submarine action in those waters. The Germans had shifted
their area of activity steadily farther south in approximately direct proportion to the intensity of the aerial defense. June 1943 saw the pattern of
sinking's moving toward the Caribbean area. By August the Gulf was practically free of sinking's which were by that time concentrated around Cuba
and in the Trinidad area. By September the enemy had given up attacks
around Cuba, Haiti and Puerto Rico, but continued in the Trinidad area
until November when a certain amount of coordination, previously lacking,
was achieved between air and surface defenses.

This progressive withdrawal of the enemy submarines does not, however, mean that the I Bomber Command had by itself made the Eastern and Gulf Sea Frontiers untenable. Its activity was a contributing, perhaps a determining factor, but it was not the only one. It appears that in the late summer of 1942 the U-boat fleet had been forced to abandon to some extent its original strategic mission of striking at Allied shipping wherever it might be found in most profitable quantities, and to have adopted a more defensive strategy dictated by Allied plans in Russia and North Africa. This shift in strategy involved greater concentrations in the northern and eastern Atlantic waters at the expense of operations in the American shipping lanes. The convoy system also did much to discourage attacks, although convoys without adequate air coverage were extremely vulnerable. And an increasingly large share of this coverage, as well as of routine patrol, was being provided by Navy planes, which accounted for 75 out of the total of 125 attacks made in the western Atlantic prior to 5 September 1943. The AAF 1st Sea Search Attack Group, operating primarily as an experimental unit from Langley Field, under the operational control of the Bomber Command, also made five successful attacks during the period from July to October. At any rate, the constant air patrol maintained by the various agencies in the antisubmarine campaign undoubtedly exercised a determining influence in the enemy's strategic withdrawal. However, the enemy had not been defeated, scarcely even embarrassed; he merely concentrated his efforts in other areas, and so effectively that in November, 2 months after he had virtually abandoned the US coastline, total Allied shipping losses reached a new high.

Steps had been taken by the Army Air Forces to increase the efficiency of its antisubmarine units. An effort had been made to increase the number of medium bombers deployed in the campaign, and to equip as many of them as possible with ASV. Above all, the Army Air Forces had established in June the Sea Search Attack Development Unit (SADU) for the purpose of research in antisubmarine techniques and devices. By August this agency was in full operation. It was through the medium of this technical development that Dr. Edward L. Bowles, Expert Consultant to the Secretary of War, hoped to revitalize the antisubmarine campaign. Considerable attention had been given to the problem of equipment, especially radar, by the Joint

Committee on New Weapons and Equipment (JNW) and it was becoming pretty evident that, if the submarines were to be defeated, some aid must be sought from these technical sources.

Unfortunately, a research unit could not win the "trade war" by itself. It was one thing to develop the weapons and quite another to use them effectively. The latter demanded a correspondingly stream-lined organization of the entire program, which meant in this instance the creation of a new command committed to an aggressive, closely knit campaign of U-boat destruction. Again the whole basic controversy was opened. It was, Dr. Bowles insisted, no longer so much a question of over-all unity of command between Army and Navy. That could well be conceded to the Navy. It was rather a question of organization within the Army itself, and for a frankly offensive campaign reaching beyond coastal patrol into the deeper waters of the mid-ocean.

He therefore proposed that an "Air Antisubmarine Force" be organized under the command of a general officer who would control the entire land-based air component of the antisubmarine forces, including the Navy land-based inshore patrol aircraft, and the research and training unit. In this way, without disturbing the ultimate unity of command, the vexing question concerning the allocation of land-based aircraft, which was tending dangerously toward the creation of two separate air forces with duplicated function, would be solved. This entire force would be placed under the Commanding General, Army Air Forces, in order to relieve it from dependency on any local command. It would confine its operations to US coastal waters, but would be free to send "detachments or task forces to other parts of the world."

The last of the major arguments that led to the establishment of the Army Air Forces Antisubmarine Command had now been presented in this penetrating document. The problem of aircraft allocations to the Army and Navy, the evident tactical need for unity of command and mobility of organization, and the Army's strategic doctrine of the coordinated offensive were all loading in an intricate and overlapping pattern of influences to the creation of a separate command. Now the requirements dictated by the employment of new devices added one more telling item to this list which, together with the continuing grave situation in the Atlantic, made action essential.

None of the plans prepared and discussed in the summer of 1942 was used as the final pattern – none, that is , in its entirety. The ideas developed in the plans, however, determined the nature of the new command. Allowance naturally had to be made for the views of the Navy which had not been favorable to the establishment of such an organization. So the solution finally adopted was a modest one, retaining most of the reforms proposed by Army planners except those specifically reducing the authority of the Navy.

The first formal step in setting up the new command was taken by General Marshall. On 14 September, he wrote to Admiral King:

```
Experience with the First Bomber Command in antisubmarine operations
since March indicates that the effective employment of air forces
against the submarine demands rapid communications, mobility, and
freedom from the restrictions inherent in command systems based upon
area responsibility.
```

Accordingly, he proposed to create the "First Antisubmarine Army Air Command," which would absorb those portions of the I Bomber Command engaged in antisubmarine work. Control of the new unit would be centralized in the War Department in order that it might "be promptly dispatched" to successive zones of submarine activity. It would begin operation in Atlantic coastal waters, the Gulf and the Caribbean; its expansion to other areas "will depend upon the planes available." Operations "naturally will be under the operational control of the sea frontier concerned." The closest cooperation with the Navy, especially in the transmission of intelligence which could only be compiled through naval sources, would be essential to the proper functioning of this antisubmarine command. Provision would therefore have to be made for liaison between "our immediate headquarters."

Admiral King replied at once, concurring in general, but expressing his belief that "the preferable method" was allocation of air units to sea frontiers, changing the allocations from time to time and from frontier to frontier as the exigencies of the war dictated. He would, he said, continue to exercise control ever Army planes through the commander of the various sea frontiers. To provide the close liaison suggested by General Marshall, he had designated Adm. P.N.L. Bellinger, Deputy Chief of Staff of the US Fleet, as liaison officer.

On 23 September, General McNarney instructed General Arnold to organize the First Antisubmarine Army Air Command, using the I Bomber Command as cadre. The principal mission of the command was to be "the location and destruction of hostile submarines." As a necessary means to this and it had the secondary mission of training crews and developing devices and techniques. The command was to be directly under the CG AAF, although operations were to be conducted under naval control. It was not to be limited by the boundaries of defense areas, and its operations in areas other than the NDC or SDC were to be coordinated with OPD, WDGS. It was activated 15 October 1942 under the designation, Army Air Forces Antisubmarine Command.

The mission of the command was elaborated in subsequent orders which gave considerable latitude to its activities. It was to attack hostile submarines "wherever they may be operating." Although operations on the Eastern and gulf Sea Frontiers were to be conducted under the tactical control of Navy officials, direct control over the command was vested in the office of the Commanding General, AAF; and provision was made for future transfer of units to extra-continental areas on a detached service base. General Larson, as Commanding General, was responsible for operations under the Director of Military Requirements, through the Director of Bombardment, but matters of "policy, broad plans, and the development of new weapons and equipment" remained with the Commanding General, AAF.

Such were the plans and orders under which the Antisubmarine Command was organized and under which it operated during the short course of its restless career.

2

THE ANTISUBMARINE CONTROVERSY

The AAF Antisubmarine Command began operations at once, and with essentially the same units and equipment as had been employed against the U-boats by its predecessor, the I Bomber Command. These squadrons were, on 20 November 1942, organized in two wings, the 25th and the 26th, with headquarters at New York and Miami, and operating in the Eastern and Gulf Sea Frontiers, respectively. Provision was made for redesignating several observation squadrons and re-equipping them for antisubmarine operations. Equipment of the I Bomber Command available for the new assignment, although including several types of aircraft, was seriously limited in the critical category of long-range bombardment. Eventually the Antisubmarine Command was to consist of 25 squadrons, most of which were equipped with B-24's, especially adapted for anti-U-boat warfare. Command headquarters remained at 90 Church St., New York City.

The command faced a large and varied problem of build-up. Not only did it have to increase its effective strength as rapidly as possible, but to meet its new obligations it had also to inaugurate an entirely new training program, new supply procedures, and now administrative machinery for coordinating research in the tactics and techniques of antisubmarine warfare. The Bomber Command had been constantly handicapped by the officially temporary nature of its assignment. The new command was able to attack its problems with all the ingenuity and energy it possessed, because it was officially committed to antisubmarine duty and had no legal reason to anticipate that at any time it might be returned to normal bombardment duties.

The command also faced the immediate necessity of extending the range of its activities beyond the western Atlantic. In November 1942, two of its squadrons, completely equipped with B-24's, were ordered to England. Later, other units were dispatched overseas, in all six squadrons doing service in the eastern Atlantic – to be specific, in the Bay of Biscay and in the Moroccan Sea Frontier. Still other units served, during 1943, in Newfoundland and in the Caribbean.

These movements were dictated by a fundamental change in German strategy for the deployment of the U-boat fleet. Indeed, the activation of the Antisubmarine Command coincided with this shift of enemy forces. Since May 1942, the Germans had been gradually withdrawing their submarine forces from the US coastal waters. By September they had apparently abandoned the policy of attacking merchant shipping wherever it might be found in profitable quantities, and had begun to concentrate their forces defensively against the military shipping which the Allies were sending to the British Isles and to Africa in preparation for offensive action in these areas. Specifically, this meant deployment in the North Atlantic and in the approaches toward North Africa. Little activity remained in the western Atlantic except in the poorly defended Trinidad area, and except for a few nuisance raiders sent to keep large antisubmarine forces tied down to patrol off the US coast. This shift of enemy strategy called for a similar shift in US strategy; and, since it was on the enemy's part essentially a shift from offense to defense, it pointed toward a corresponding change in American policy from defense to a vigorous offense. Even if this natural logic were ignored, the new situation made a greatly expanded antisubmarine campaign absolutely essential.

The new submarine situation thus necessitated a review of antisubmarine measures. Old questions regarding the strategy and organization of the antisubmarine campaign, never satisfactorily settled, began again to render unstable the relationship between the services and to imperil a vital sector of the Allied war effort. It again became a crucial question whether the extended antisubmarine war should proceed an essentially offensive lines, carrying the battle to the enemy as briskly as resources would permit, or whether it should consist primarily of extended convey coverage. And it again became a subject for the most heated debate whether the long-range, land-based aviation engaged in the campaign should be controlled ultimately by the Army or by the Navy.

The creation of the Antisubmarine Command, then, settled nothing. It had the effect of substantially legalizing the Army's antisubmarine mission, hitherto considered exclusively a naval one, entrusted to the Army only as a temporary emergency measure. But it reconciled none of these differences of opinion which had harassed the antisubmarine campaign from the very beginning. On both the strategic and the administrative level, the newly aggravated debate led inevitable toward a crisis in the summer of 1943 which, in turn, affected the entire system of joint action and, incidentally, removed the Antisubmarine Command entirely from the scene.

Although the command had been conceived originally as a unit whose permanent field of operations should be the US Atlantic coast, the Gulf, and the Caribbean, it did not take the War Department long to recognize the need for extending its activities beyond the western Atlantic. General Marshall had, in fact, hinted at the possibility of extending the scope of the Army's antisubmarine forces in his letter of 14 September. Dr. Bowles had urged the possibility of extra continental expansion in his memo of 7 August, and apparently he had the support of General Eisenhower. General Arnold, and Secretary Stimson in this point of view. As conceived by General Arnold and presented to the Joint Chiefs of Staff in JCS 93/1 (dated 19 October 1942), "The unit (the newly activated command) had freedom of action in that it may be moved to where it is most needed, and operate in conjunction with but met under the command of the local sector commander." And in December the scope of its operations was officially widened to include the destruction of submarines "wherever they may be operating in opposition to our war effort." Plans had natured, by October, to send two squadrons to England to operate with the Coastal Command, and, on 2 November the first unit left Langley Field. The Joint Chiefs of Staff had approved a plan for considerable extended antisubmarine operation in which 416 AAF bombardment aircraft (238 heavy and 128 medium) were set as the forces to be made available for this task.

These figures, though representing a greatly enlarged program failed to satisfy General Larson whose ideas were shaped on an even broader pattern. To be sure, the forces immediately at hand were, as he put it on 6 January 1943, still too small to allow him to fulfill the mission with which he was officially charged. They consisted of 19 squadrons operating 209 planes, of which only 20 were B-24's, the type already recognized as the best available weapon for the purpose. Interpreting his mission literally, General Larson on that date presented to General Arnold a plan providing for the creation of antisubmarine wings to operate in the North Atlantic, the United Kingdom, Northwest Africa, the Mediterranean, Central West Africa, South Africa, Natal, the Antilles, the Pacific Coast, the Northwest Pacific, the Southwest Pacific, India, Asia, Hawaii, and Russia. Owing to the relative mobility of antisubmarine units, he felt that "for initial planning" the mission could be accomplished by expanding the Antisubmarine Command to a strength less than half that required to maintain squadrons in all possible areas. He therefore requested that the AAF Antisubmarine Command be authorized a total strength of six wings composing a total number of 43 squadrons. In order to equip these units, a total of 544 B-24D aircraft, fully equipped for antisubmarine activity, would be required. He further requested that the recommendations be approved in principle regardless of whether the means of implementing them were available.

AAF Headquarters approved this plan in principle with, among others, one major exception. The Antisubmarine Command was intended to be "a highly mobile striking force" which at no time would "become confined to a stabilized effort" but would operate "where operation is most profitable." With this in mind it had bee limited to 20 heavy and 4 medium squadrons, not including such as might be transferred to the command and be re-designated as antisubmarine squadrons. Immediate requirements were placed at 228 B-24's, 13 for each of the existing 19 squadrons. In the absence of fully adequate forces, these that were available had to be utilized to the utmost, which involved rapid movement from one threatened area to another. In other words, mobility was considered essential not only to the tactical and strategic situations, but to the logistical as well.

This plan for expansion implied a doctrine of the strategic offensive. It was based on the notion that the job of the Antisubmarine Command was not more protection of shipping but an organized U-boat hunt, aiming ultimately at destroying the submarine at sea. The Antisubmarine Command was not alone in this crusade for the offensive. In January, Dr. P. M. Morse, of the Antisubmarine Warfare Operations Research Group (ASWORG), analyzed the situation in the following terms:

> ... a major change in the antisubmarine battle requires that we pass from the defensive to the offensive. The plane is primarily an offensive weapon against U-boats; being preeminent, by reason of its speed, in its ability to seek out the enemy. The surface vessel is, at present, less than one tenth as efficient at finding submarines as is the plane and is no more efficient at killing the submarine, once found. Its major advantage over the plane is its staying power, essentially a defensive property: the surface vessel will always be the backbone of the convoy escort. The plane is also useful as an escort; but it is a most inefficient use of the plane's offensive capabilities to hold it down to protecting convoys which are not specifically threatened.

Moreover, like General Larson, Dr. Morse looked to a vastly increased aerial campaign, going so far as to say that 1,000 to 2,000 long-range aircraft would be necessary in the total antisubmarine war if that effort were to result in eliminating the U-boat. The Bay of Biscay and the North African coast had, he said, at the time (5 January 1943), the highest submarine density of any portion of the North Atlantic. He therefore strongly urged the Antisubmarine Command to provide enough planes to carry on offensive operations in these areas.

A similar attitude was taken about the same time by the Joint US Committee on New Weapons and Equipment. This agency complained of the naval policy which employed AAF antisubmarine aircraft chiefly in convey escort and in patrol of waters that had been practically free of submarines for months. For, although two units (ultimately organized as the 480th Antisubmarine Group) had been allowed to operate under the RAF Coastal Command in a campaign of search and attack in areas of high submarine density, the bulk of the AAFAC squadrons remained in the US coastal frontiers from which the enemy had long since withdrawn the bulk of his forces. It advocated extending the idea of "special groups with the specific task of killing submarines." These, it claimed, "might well reduce substantially the number of enemy submarines operating." The AAFAC was, it continued, such a group, and it recommended that the command be provided with an adequate supply of long-range planes and sent out in an offensive U-boat hunt.

From other sources, however, came certain qualifications to these somewhat enthusiastic statements of the offensive concept. Brig. Gen. C.W. Russell, Army liaison officer for antisubmarine warfare, had, in November, made an analysis of the situation in the Atlantic and had come up with a modified faith in the "killer-hunt" idea. Certain points rose obtrusively to the surface in his report. One was that the number of U-boats would have to be reduced before shipping losses would permanently decline. However carefully the convoys might be protected, he said, "the inescapable fact is that the more submarines there are operating, the more merchant vessels will be sunk." The second fact was that present defensive operations against the U-boat had failed to hold shipping losses "within tolerable limits." It seemed therefore that "persistent offensive measures" would have to be adopted, aimed at destroying the U-boat fleet. But General Russell was not at all sure that action in the open sea was the type of offensive required. Although, he complained, many attacks were being made on the enemy craft at sea, both by air and surface craft, few had met with success. Equipment fell short of the lethal requirements to kill many U-boats and the latter had the advantage of a highly protective element. Accordingly, while not scorning the part played by long-range bombers operating at sea, he placed in first priority the yards at which the submarines were built.

In January he repeated his recommendation, citing what he believed to be the effective bombing by Eighth Air Force units of French Coast submarine bases. He added, however, that the North Atlantic convoy route indicated the crying need for long-range, land-based aircraft, losses having "invariably" occurred in sections of the convoy route not provided with air coverage. And he advised that the AAFAC be equipped with long-range aircraft at the earliest possible moment. In short, bombing of submarine yards should be given first priority, and long-range air coverage for the North Atlantic convoy route a close second.

A summary of the official AAF policy, formulated 6 February 1943, reflected General Russell's point of view, if anything reducing the emphasis he had placed on long-range air coverage:

```
In considering the entire antisubmarine problem (General Stratemeyer
wrote), it is desired to emphasize that use of aircraft and surface
forces against submarines at sea can never be expected to effectively
reduce the total number of operational submarines. The only way to
destroy the submarines is to destroy them at their source by destruction
of crucial materials, assembly plants, yards and operating bases. Any
diversion of a large submarines at sea, would be reducing the effective
number which can be used against the submarines at their source and is
an improper employment of available forces; however, it must also be
borne in mind that unless we do protect our shipping, we will be unable
to feed and supply forces now committed to the theaters … We must,
there fore, divert a certain amount of our effort to protection of our
lines of communication. The amount so diverted should be sufficient only
to fill the need of protecting our shipping and not sufficient to
attempt to destroy the submarine at sea.
```

It would appear that AAF headquarters was admittedly groping in its effort to assign an unquestionable priority to any one type of air antisubmarine operation. A study had been requested which would indicate, in the light of recent experience, the relative effectiveness of attacking submarine production, repair and maintenance installations, parts manufacturing plants, and the operating submarines themselves. Early in March an exhaustive, if still necessarily tentative, study was submitted by AC/AS, Intelligence. By that time merchant vessel sinking's had taken a sharp upward turn, and emphasis was being placed on immediate results. This report concluded (1) that air patrols, either by land or carrier-based planes, can materially reduce shipping losses, even without a high rate of submarines "killed"; (2) that improved weapons may be expected to raise the lethal rate of aircraft attacks; (3) that bombing of submarine bases and construction yards, though still unproved, should be pressed – the bombing of component parts plants could not, however, be expected to yield large results. This report, then, while not destroying faith in the offensive of the Eighth Air Force against the submarines at their source, renewed somewhat the official confidence in an aggressive sea-search-attack policy. It pointed to the belief that the effect of air patrol could not be measured entirely in terms of U-boats sunk. It was, in fact, quite possible to limit submarine action simply by such harrying tactics as had recently been employed in the Bay of Biscay where antisubmarine forces, although sinking relatively few of the U-bombs attacked, had managed to give the enemy craft such a bad time, both in going from and returning to their bases, that their effectiveness in convoy areas was sharply reduced. This report also highlighted what had frequently been mentioned as a major criticism of the over-all US antisubmarine policy, namely that a large proportion of the Antisubmarine Command strength was left tied to a coastal patrol area, flying thousand of hours where few if any submarines were operating, while only limited forces were being moved to those areas, the Bay of Biscay for example, where the submarines abounded.

In general, the Army Air forces advocated an increased air effort in which bombing of submarine bases, air coverage for convoys, and an independent air offensive where the U-boats were thickest, each had its peculiar function, not to be overrated. Perhaps the Antisubmarine Command stressed the last policy because it was its own; but even it was satisfied with any strategic policy which carried the war as directly and as rapidly as possible to the enemy, considering, of course, commitments of equal or higher priority. Its planners were apparently quite agreed that continued emphasis should be placed on striking the U-boats in their construction yards and operating bases. Yet it was on the question of independent offensive action in areas of enemy concentration that one of the decisive controversies became focused.

Early in 1943, during February, German submarines began their spring offensive. Merchant vessel sinking's, after having decreased rapidly during December and January, suddenly increased, especially along the North Atlantic convoy route. This renewed activity called for drastic measures, but there was considerable room for disagreement as to what these measures should be. Given unlimited supplies of trained men and specialized equipment, both sides might easily have justified their respective measures, each as part of a many-sided, coordinated campaign. But, as usual, the plans were numerous and the equipment meager. Naval authorities, continuing to invest their hopes in an extended system of convoy coverage, stressed the need for more Army B-24's operating from Newfoundland in order to cover that hitherto especially dangerous leg of the journey from US ports to Europe. The AAFAC, without doubting for a moment the need for this activity from Newfoundland — even, in fact, planning experimental operations from Greenland as well – nevertheless felt that a considerable portion of its available strength in VLR aircraft should be devoted to an independent offensive.

Since November 1943, the Coastal command, RAF had been carrying on just such an offensive against the U-boat in its transit area in the Bay of Biscay. The Bay was a focal area through which virtually all the enemy operating in the Atlantic had to pass as they left or approached their bases on the west coast of France. This campaign, therefore, became not only the pivot on which the RAF turned its antisubmarine war, but the archetype of a VLR air killer offensive. In November two AAFAC squadrons had been sent to England, with the original mission of protecting TORCH convoys. After consultation with the British, the Commanding General, ETO decided to employ these squadrons in the Bay of Biscay to augment the Coastal Command's effort, because that organization had a very limited supply of ASV-10 equipment (the sine qua non for effective U-boat hunting). These two squadrons accordingly took an active part in the "Gondola" campaign, 6-15 February 1943, which marked one of the high points of the Biscay offensive.

The Biscay campaign failed, however, to impress Admiral King who felt that, although "excellent in concept," it had been pushed with a vigor unwarranted by "diminishing returns," and which might better have been expended on the Newfoundland area. Submarine sightings had, he complained, become steadily ewer in the Bay of Biscay, by February no more than one for each 250 hours of flying, while German submarines had been allowed to concentrate and flourish with little interference off the Newfoundland banks "for several months." He appreciated the fact that the AAFAC had "the Newfoundland matter" now in hand. What gave him concern was "the length of time it took to make the picture clear." To this criticism, the AAFAC replied that the Biscay offensive was one which would require continual air effort to restrict U-boat operations; that an increase in the number of hours per sighting was a favorable sign since it indicated that the enemy submarines, which were evidently increasing in number, were having to traverse the Biscay transit area under conditions which could only reduce their efficiency. Furthermore, the recent U-boat concentrations in the North Atlantic were being reported beyond effective range from the Newfoundland air bases. They could be reached from Greenland, and plans were being laid to operate from there with at least on VLR squadron; but operating conditions were so bad in that area that little could be expected from such action. In fine, "Our conception of this problem is that the protection of the sea lanes is basically a Navy problem," and AAFAC units are better employed in the specialized work for which they were specially trained and equipped – specifically, such operations as these in the Bay of Biscay.

And so the discussion developed. Mainly it was a case of emphasis, rather than of mutually exclusive views. As an Eighth Air Force report put it, "The air war against the U-boats should not be regarded as either wholly defensive, nor wholly offensive. It can probably best be termed a counter-offensive." It was also very difficult to prove, conclusively, either argument. It was against this operational and doctrinal background that the Atlantic Convoy Conference met in Washington, from 1 to 12 March 1943, comprising representatives from British, Canadian, and US agencies concerned in the Battle of the Atlantic. Among several other topics, this of the proper deployment of VLR land-based aircraft rose stubbornly to the surface during the deliberations of the conference.

By this time it had become generally recognized that antisubmarine warfare was a problem for air power just as much as for surface forces, if not considerable more. Much time was still being spent in documenting this point and the operational statistics regarding attacks and sinking's of enemy submarines tended to move steadily in favor of aircraft. And it was equally evident that too few aircraft, especially VLR, were being employed in this kind of warfare. Admiral Noble, R.W., struck this note early in the conference:

```
The submarine menace, to my mind, is becoming every day more and more an
air problem. We haven't had enough aircraft during the last two years.
We are just reaching a point where we can see ahead of us the chance of
getting enough, and I am sure this conference will come to some
agreements and decisions as to how to best use these aircraft when we
get them and when they get to their proper operational theaters.
```

The Atlantic Convoy Conference, however, dealt only with the problem of air coverage for convoys, insofar as air operations were included in its recommendations at all. The problem of an air offensive was ignored, no doubt, for the very good reason that it bore only indirectly on the problem of convoy. Admiral King, however, took pains in his opening address as chairman to make his position on this subject very clear:

I take upon myself the privilege of offering some advice as to how you should go at the matters in hand … the High Command recognizes that the antisubmarine war is a matter of first importance; but we must also recognize that the defeat of the U-boat is not of itself the goal we seek, however much it is an essential step in reaching the goal. May I add the observation that your immediate task is to protect our shipping by what may be called defensive antisubmarine warfare … We have got to devote our somewhat limited overall resources only in part to fighting the submarines. This makes it necessary that we use what we have to the very best advantage … I have heard something about "killer groups" which may be of great use when we can get enough means, provided they are used directly in connection with the convoy routes, for that is where the "bait" is. I see no profit in searching the ocean, or even any but a limited area, such as a focal area – all else puts to shame the proverbial "search for a needle in a haystack" … antisubmarine warfare for the remainder of 1943, at least, must concern itself primarily with the escort of convoys.

In these words, Admiral King recommitted himself, if not the entire US Navy, to a policy of defense in the U-boat war, at least for the rest of the year. Yet at the same time he left the way open for the future development of an offensive strategy.

Concurrently with this debate regarding strategic doctrine ran a parallel debate concerning organization. The controversy over strategy suggested that some reorganization of command would alone be likely to remedy a basic disagreement over the deployment of forces. The nature of the antisubmarine war remained such as to demand as nearly absolute cooperation between the commands and services involved as was humanly possible. And there were other problems which pointed in the same direction. All boil down in the final analysis to the constant need for economy and for mobility in the use of those resources available.

It was the old story over again, reminiscent of the days before the AAFAC was activated. The German submarine fleet, under a single commander, and deployed within a large strategic plan, possessed the great advantage of flexibility; and being flexible it was able to retain the initiative in the Atlantic even after it had been forced by strategic considerations beyond its control to concentrate its efforts defensively against the "invasion" convoys. In contrast, the antisubmarine forces, especially those of the United States, suffered from complicated and divided command and from a wasteful duplication of effort. Little attempt had been made to standardize communications, intelligence dissemination, training, or tactical doctrine, either among the nations concerned or between the US Army and the US Navy. As a consequence, each agency felt that, in order to discharge its obligation, it would have to plan a much larger program than would have been required in a strictly integrated plan. Finally, no single commander existed, either among the Allies or within the US forces, whose sole responsibility it was to prosecute antisubmarine warfare, and to move antisubmarine forces as the tactical situation indicated.

Although it was a problem involving the entire campaign and each of the Atlantic Allies, it was a particularly aggravated form. Basic disagreement existed concerning the nature of the antisubmarine mission. Each service seems to have planned with the entire campaign in mind – AAF authorities had observed with some misgivings that the navy was including in its allocation plans a force sufficient to do the whole job without the aid of the AAFAC. This duplication, or threat thereof, involved training facilities and bases as well as planes. Though the Navy exercised operational control over all US antisubmarine operations, it had as yet no integrated system for exercising that control. The job was left to the various sea frontier commanders who had other responsibilities, under the coordinating authority of the Commander in Chief, US Fleet, whose office had also many other things to do. And the AAFAC, organized, equipped, and trained under the administration of the AAF, actually failed to fit into this inflexible system of naval control. The result was that the AAFAC flyers had frequently to work with naval commanders who did not understand their training, equipment or tactical doctrine. Still worse, units of valuable antisubmarine aircraft were left frozen to naval frontier commands where practically no submarines existed or to the protection of "unthreatened" convoys, while certain overseas waters teemed with the enemy. It was alleged that the Navy not only failed to act upon over-all intelligence reports concerning U-boat concentrations, but failed also to provide the AAFAC units with enough basic intelligence data upon which to operate effective patrols. The position of the overseas squadrons (the two sent to England in November of 1942 and moved to Africa in March 1943) was especially anomalous. Without wing organization in which they might have found some degree of autonomy, these squadrons were forced to operate under a foreign (although basically congenial) system while in England, and while in Africa under a bitterly disputed area command. Any attempt to move the AAFAC squadrons involved ponderous procedures within War and Navy department channels, possibly even unavoidable slow liaison with other Allied commands. The result was that movements were likely to be too slow to cope with the extreme mobility of the U-boat fleet.

Most agencies concerned recognized the need for reorganization of the antisubmarine effort. Admiral King, himself no friend of radical change, experienced impatience at the slowness with which the antisubmarine forces were being moved to counter the shifting U-boat concentrations. And he had agreed, a little grudgingly, to General Marshall's proposal that a study be undertaken to improve coordination in the campaign. The problem was accordingly entrusted to a sub-committee of the Combined Staff Planners (created 3 January 1943) for study and recommendation.

Preliminary discussions in the subcommittee seem to have been promising. The flaws in existing organization, especially the lack of unified command, were too obvious to excite much disagreement in the abstract. According to the AAF members, however, it appears that on second thought the US Navy members "interposed strenuous objections" to any plan which amounted to a change in their existing organization or policies. The result was a paper which the AAF members felt "intimates much but specifically says nothing."

What this report (CPS 56/3, dated 1 March 1943) did was to present the problem formally and collect considerable reference data on the problem of countering the submarine menace. Little exception could be taken by anyone to the general recommendations concerning organization. It recommended that the national antisubmarine effort in each Allied nation be integrated under one naval commander who "should be able to concentrate entirely on that task." Forces should be allocated to antisubmarine operations exclusively and areas of operation clearly defined, especially for the air forces of the two services. To permit flexibility in control and operation,

"an ideal to be aimed at" would be the creation of a system of bases, communications, and weather-forecasting facilities within which the forces might be moved rapidly from one area to another. Although a single authority for the total United Nations antisubmarine effort would be very desirable, that would have to visit until the national organizations became more uniform with each other, a process which would take time. Meanwhile, with increased flexibility and augmented forces, it would be reasonable to expect the antisubmarine machine to be set to work on both offensive and defensive projects in which air and surface forces would operate in close cooperation.

Innocuous as this report appears, it aroused vigorous protest on the part of the AAF members. After much discussion, during which the recommendations had been considerable diluted, they had agreed to sign it rather than to submit a split paper. Colonel Williamson did, however, turn in a minority report in which he objected that the subcommittee had given too little attention to reducing the number of U-boats at sea. He recommended that first priority be given to implementing plans for organizational and technical developments which would increase the effectiveness of action against the submarines at sea, including the use of killer groups composed of radar and DF-equipped destroyers to break up submarine concentrations. There should, he maintained, be no diversion from offensive operations to defensive convoy coverage.

The AAF members further clarified their position in a plan of their own for reorganizing the antisubmarine machinery, which they submitted to General Arnold. They proposed specifically that each of the major Allied nations concerned should create a task force under a single commander who should control all national anti-U-boat operations; that all national air and surface forces (the latter including carriers) be placed under an air and surface commander respectively; that all Allied antisubmarine forces in the Atlantic be placed under one commander who would have no other responsibility; and that this over-all commander should be given a deputy for air and one for surface forces operating in the Atlantic. This statement represented the AAFAC position in general, and was in substantial agreement with the British and Canadian opinion. An earlier plan from AAFAC sources had made no objection to leaving supreme control in naval hands "since the responsibility for securing trade routes is the responsibility of the Commander-in-Chief of the Navy." The official AAFAC position was thus less radical than some earlier recommendations, such as that submitted in January 1943 by the Joint US Committee on New Weapons and Equipment which would have removed the AAFAC entirely from the control of the Navy, and made it into a specialized force for locating and destroying U-boats wherever the latter might be found.

The report of the CPS subcommittee (CPS 56/3) continued to be discussed. In general it was felt to be a useful report, lacking, however, in recommendations of a sufficiently specific nature to be of much value in actual planning. An CCS 203, it was submitted to the Joint Chiefs of Staff and the Combined Chiefs of Staff, and on 20 April 1943, after almost 6 months of discussion, it was decided that this document should be approved in principle and sent to the agencies concerned for "guidance" and "appropriate action." Action in any greater detail had been forestalled by Admiral King who feared that, if the CCS approved the paper in its entirety, the result would be to restrict rather than to improve antisubmarine operations. Throughout these deliberations, Admiral King seems to have been especially concerned to avoid any sort of agreement which would limit the autonomy of the US Navy, by taking from it the right to reorganize the forces under its responsibility according to its own plans.

This same attitude had been apparent when, in the meantime, the Atlantic Convoy Conference met early in March, to ponder the extremely critical situation in the North Atlantic. Short of making clearer the areas of national responsibility in the convoy routes, this conference avoided the ticklish question of organization. Admiral King, its chairman, had warned against what he felt would be an unnecessarily unsettling discussion on that point. He appealed to the conference for "unification of effort," but added:

```
May I caution you not to think that unity of command is a panacea for
all military difficulties. Unity of Command in appropriate circumstances
does unify the effort, but inappropriate centralization of command
produces only the form and not the substance of unified effort.
```

He warned especially of "mixed forces," a comment which surprised Air Marshal Durston, who spoke very favorable of the cooperation achieved by the RAF Coastal Command and the AAFAC squadrons sent to the United Kingdom.

During the spring of 1943, then, the problem of organization was being weighed without more result than an uneasy agreement that some reform, in the direction of closer integration of authority, would be highly desirable. Meanwhile the rugged logic of events was fast outrunning the more academic thinking that prevailed in the official conferences. By March the situation in the North Atlantic had become so grave that President Roosevelt, on the 18th, wrote as follows to the Chief of Staff, US Army and the Commander in chief, US Fleet:

Since the rate of sinking of our merchant ships in the North Atlantic during the past week has increased at a rate that threatens seriously the security of Great Britain, and therefore both "Husky" and "Bolero," it seems evident that every available weapon must be used at once to counteract the enemy submarine campaign.

Both Army and navy high commands had come to about the same conclusion, and every effort was being made to strengthen the antisubmarine striking force. The AAFAC squadrons formerly operating from England were moved, In March, to Ft. Lyautey in North Africa to help cover the vital approaches to that theater. In accordance with the recommendations of the Atlantic Convoy Conference, additional squadrons were made available for Newfoundland to help cover that critical leg of the northern convoy route. General Arnold had declared himself especially anxious to implement the ACC recommendations in their two areas as quickly as possible. In order to supply the necessary VLR aircraft for this increased ocean coverage, the Combined Chiefs of Staff committed their respective nations to provide, by 1 July 1943, planes of this type according to the following schedule:

US AAF	75
US Naval AF	60
RAF	105
RCAF	15
	255

General Arnold left no doubt about the "firmness" of this commitment. Fortunately, it was estimated that it could be met without changing planned commitments to other theaters.

What remained to be done was to make the antisubmarine machinery, thus fueled, to operate both effectively and economically. Reorganization would raise basic issues, many of which had proved chronically insoluble. But something had to be done to remedy what was now recognized as the bottleneck of the Allied war effort in the West. In this spirit, General Marshall wrote to Admiral King on 16 April:

```
I wish to state now that I feel the air operations against submarines
can be greatly improved and that complete reorganization of method,
particularly as applies to very long range aircraft, is plainly
indicated … . We (Generals Marshall, Arnold, and Hellerney) are all
firmly of the opinion that the present procedure is largely ineffective
and makes poor use of a valuable instrument.
```

And it was in this spirit that brought the matter before the Joint Chiefs of Staff 3 days later.

War Department experts had meanwhile been at work on plans for reorganizing the antisubmarine effort, insofar as it involved the use of VLR and LR aircraft. It had become evident that this was the crux of the entire problem, overshadowing, in its immediacy, the loftier issue of unified Allied control. It was on the basis of these studies that General Marshall was prepared to take action in the Joint Chiefs of Staff.

Early in March, Dr. Bowles, who had remained throughout its history the sage of the antisubmarine program, and had worked in the closest relationship with Secretary Stimson, submitted an exhaustive report to the Secretary of War covering the entire submarine situation. In it he set forth what may be termed the logical Army policy with regard to the control of the AAFAC. His recommendations arose from certain fundamental assumptions: (1) that the problem of antisubmarine warfare, since on it depended the Army mission in Europe, was essentially an Army problem; (2) that offensive tactics, both against the submarines' breeding grounds and on the open sea, could alone reduce the submarine fleet and therefore the mounting menace to vital Allied shipping; (3) that the long range land-based bomber is the most useful weapon in this offensive strategy; and (4) that an effective use of this weapon depended on a closely coordinated and independent antisubmarine command. Together, these assumptions led to certain inescapable conclusions concerning organization. First of all, antisubmarine forces, whether surface-craft or aircraft, Army or Navy, should be consolidated under one head, who should have the freedom of action and the status of a theater commander. The man to whom the responsibility would be entrusted for the safety of supply to the overseas troops should naturally be an Army man. "The U-boat is primarily a weapon against supply, not against naval fleets."

Since "past difficulties have in no small measure stemmed from a failure to realize the effectiveness of air attack on the U-boat," the new commander and the new organization should be such that the air arm would enjoy the greatest possible mobility and freedom of initiative. Although effective enough in the past, new weapons and navigational aids should, if used intelligently, make future operations against the submarine decisively successful. In order to eliminate the necessity of routing commands through AAF channels – coordination of the Army antisubmarine program was then being accomplished through the Director of Bombardment – Dr. Bowles suggested placing the AAFAC under the direct control of Operations Division, WD General Staff, with theater status.

Dr. Bowles expressed some concern that such a large proportion of B-24 production was being allocated to the Navy, since most of these precious "heavies" would become a part of the Navy's own antisubmarine force on the Atlantic Coast. "Could we not," he urged, "make more efficient use of them in our own Command?" and, moreover, "should not a duplication of effort be discouraged?"

Secretary Stimson gave Dr. Bowles' study his approval. He was especially pleased with the prospect that under the proposed plan the Army could have an attacking system in operation by midsummer rather than by the end of the year, which was the best the Navy could offer under its current plans. He foresaw difficulties in coordinating with the Navy, and he was prepared to take the matter to the President if that service proved "too obdurate in respect to cooperation." In any event he was opposed to a compromise treatment of these plans in the Joint Chiefs of Staff which would "not allow full operational freedom to the Army in the command of killer planes."

Such a compromise (he wrote on 14 March 1943) might stultify the vigor and initiative available through the faith and initiative of our air command. There is a very good precedent for such freedom in the British relation between the coastal Command and the British Admiralty. We ought to strike at no less than that.

Planners within the AAFAC followed roughly the lines of policy suggested by Dr. Bowles. Apparently recognizing the fact that, until some final settlement of the command question could be reached, a period of experimental operations would have to be gone through, they proposed two alternate plans to allow units of the command to operate through the AAF chain of command and not "under the operational control of any other headquarters." According to Plan A, the CG, AAFAC would deploy all his units in any required areas, operations to be conducted in cooperation with whatever air and surface antisubmarine forces might be active in these areas, but, presumably, not under the control of any such forces. According to Plan B he would create a task force composed of certain designated units of the Command which would operate on a status similar to that of Plan A, the reminder of the units operating as they were at that date, under operational control of the Navy.

The Secretary of War had, a few days earlier (1 April 1943), made a proposal similar to Plan B. As a temporary stopgap measure he suggested the organization of a small task force within the AAFAC to function "during the experimental period more or less in an independent status." The Secretary of the Navy had given his veto and that of COMINCH to this plan which they felt to be tactically unsound.

With reference to these abortive discussions, and on the basis of plane outlined by War Department experts, General Marshall frankly raised the issue of organization in the Joint Chiefs of Staff. In a memorandum (JCS 268), presented on 19 April 1943, he declared himself strongly of the opinion that the ultimate solution for the employment of the air arm in antisubmarine operations "particularly, and possibly exclusively as applied to VLR aircraft" could only be found in a unified command responsible for that type of operations. If such an authority could be set up, the result would be to override the limiting effect of the system of naval districts and sea frontiers under which the air arm had been forced to operate. If such authority could not be determined, he felt "we will tend to limp along under unavoidable difficulties that always exist when a new procedure has to develop under normal staff routine and operational organization." He therefore proposed that the US shore-based air forces on antisubmarine duty in the Atlantic be organized to provide "highly mobile striking forces" for offensive action in addition to convoy coverage "in certain critical areas," and that this command operate directly under JCS as to policy in a manner similar to that of a theater commander. Moreover, in view of the urgency of the situation, General Marshall added that the Army and Navy should each provide VLR B-24's for this command at the rate of 12 per month during May, June, and July – this in addition to the 75 Army and 60 Navy VLR aircraft currently allocated to the antisubmarine campaign.

In JCS 268, General Marshall hoped to place the joint air force above questions of rival jurisdiction. By vesting the control of his proposed command in the JCS themselves, with COMINCH as their executive, he left the way open for the appointment by JCS of an immediate commander most suitable for the job. It was a solution more in accord with the complex and competing command relationships than Dr. Bowles', though no more logical than the latter's proposal that final authority rest with the War Department. According to policy then in the process of formulation (JCS 263/2/ D, dated 20 April 1943), command of any joint force would be settled on the basis of the nature of the mission to be performed, and the single commander would be designated by the Joint Chiefs of Staff. Now it did not take abnormal insight to see that in view of this policy a very strong argument could and would be made for an Army Air Forces officer as commander of the VLR aircraft on antisubmarine duty. For the moment, General Marshall was apparently willing to leave that point unstated, hoping that, as soon as JCS 263/2/D was approved the question would resolve itself.

Navy authorities no doubt arrived at this conclusion themselves, for action on JCS 268 was deferred pending the receipt of a report being prepared by the Navy Department bearing on the same problem. On 1 May, Admiral King presented his alternative plan (JCS 263/1, dated 3 May

1943). He proposed to set up at once in the Navy Department an antisubmarine command to be known as the Tenth Fleet. Headquarters of this command would consist of "all existing antisubmarine activities of the US Fleet." The Commander, Tenth Fleet, would have direct command over all sea frontiers, using frontier commanders as task force commanders; and he would exercise control over all LR and VLR aircraft engaged in the work. In order to avoid duplication, initial training in Army antisubmarine aviation would be given by the AAFAC under guiding directives prepared by the Commander, Tenth Fleet. Maintenance of any antisubmarine aviation would also appropriately remain a function of the Commanding General, AAF. A logistical plan would be evolved to permit the greatest possible mobility on the part of the air units.

The Tenth Fleet proposal provided only a partial answer to the problem. It vested responsibility for antisubmarine operations in a commander who did not have competing claims to his attention. That at least was a step in the right direction. But it did not in any way meet General Marshall's recommendations in JCS 238. It placed shore-based air power under the control of the Navy Department rather than the JCS; and, while it appeared to involve a sweeping reorganization of the Navy Department, it actually did nothing of the sort, for it left the system of sea frontier commands as the basic machinery for the employment of the air arm. Indeed, to AAF observers it seemed that the only real change involved in Admiral King's paper was that COMINCH would emerge with increased control over AAF antisubmarine forces and the right to use Army bases. It also appeared that Admiral King envisaged the possible expansion of the Tenth Fleet's jurisdiction beyond the Atlantic to include the South and Southwest Pacific. This jurisdiction would actually involve the authority to allocate antisubmarine aircraft and vessels between Atlantic and Pacific areas, a prerogative hitherto resting with the JCS.

Final action on the Tenth Fleet proposal (JCS 268/1) was left to personal discussion between Admiral King, General Marshall, and General Arnold. Although the plan failed to meet his full approval, General Marshall was willing to compromise. He recognized that, according to JCS 263/2/D, the Navy had prior interest in antisubmarine warfare in general. He was therefore willing to accept the Tenth Fleet even at the expense of removing antisubmarine operations from the province of the JCS to that of the Navy Department. And since the air component would be a joint force it should be operated within the Tenth Fleet. But JCS 263/2/D would also govern the command of this joint land-based air force. Not only was the antisubmarine mission of special importance to the Army, but the problems of bases, air transport, maintenance, and supply were all essentially Army problems. And, with some 400 VLR bombers scheduled for this antisubmarine mission by the end of the year, the Army was entitled to some recognition in the command organization. General Marshall therefore requested that an Army air officer be given command of the VLR and LR aircraft engaged in antisubmarine warfare. It is impossible to determine from the available papers how this request was received. It is clear, however, that on 19 May, Admiral King proclaimed the existence of the Tenth Fleet, under the direct command of COMINCH, for the purpose of exercising unity of control over US antisubmarine operations in that part of the Atlantic under US strategic control.

The Tenth Fleet, though a step in the right direction, solved nothing. The situation remained in an acute state of unstable equilibrium. In fact, it may be that, by the latter part of May, a compromise settlement on the antisubmarine situation was no longer possible. By that time, an issue much larger than that of the land-based antisubmarine air force had been raised, and a solution of the lesser problem would have to wait until the larger issue, of which it constituted a part, could be satisfactorily settled. In other words, control of land-based antisubmarine aircraft raised the question of the control of all land-based long-range aircraft employed on overwater missions.

The Navy had steadfastly resisted the notion that land-based aviation constituted a virtually separate arm which no longer fitted into the older pattern of the two primary services. In a perfectly natural effort to make its forces self-contained and to be as free as possible from the cramping necessity of coordinating with forces of another service over which it could exercise only an indirect authority, the Navy had striven to build up an air force of its own. This effort became especially vigorous when the long- and very-long-range land-based bombing plane demonstrated its prominence in the execution of long-distance offshore patrol. The Navy quickly recognized the value of the B-24 and secured large allocations of these aircraft. By the end of June 1943, the Navy had received almost its full quota of 60 ASV-equipped VLR aircraft specifically designated for antisubmarine operations, and was requesting increased allocations for patrol work in other theaters. According to the Bureau of Aeronautics, this requirement for an increase in land-based aircraft arose in part from a shift of emphasis from seaplanes to long- and medium-range land planes for both antisubmarine operations in the Atlantic, and sea-search, reconnaissance, and patrols in the Pacific. And Admiral King had, in his comments on the unified antisubmarine command, intimated that he hoped such a system could be extended to include operations in the Pacific.

It was a very natural policy on the part of a service which had traditionally maintained a purity of organization impossible in the Army forces. As General Marshall pointed out, the problem of control of long-range aircraft operating with the Navy on antisubmarine patrol bore a marked similarity to the Army problem of divisional organization. A divisional commander knows that he can handle the artillery and engineers more efficiently if they are all organic parts of the division and do not include elements attached only for a particular operation. But, without forces almost unlimited in numbers, such a policy would result in a duplication which, however efficient for the particular project, would be ruinously wasteful to the war effort as a whole. This was a problem which the Army had been forced to face since 1917. But, except for the creation of virtually a second army in the shape of the Marines, the problem had not presented itself to the Navy until the question of air striking forces had arisen. It was a trend which, if carried to its logical conclusion, would mean the eventual consolidation of the Army and Navy, for it would remove the essential distinction between them.

It is clear that the Navy had no such consolidation in mind. But for some time, in fact from the beginning of the allocation of B-24 aircraft to the Navy, Army observers had been concerned about the Navy's plans for controlling these forces. Now, in the summer of 1943, it began to appear that the Navy was bent, not only on building up a large force of long-range land-based bombers for patrol purposes and convoy coverage, but was prepared as well to deploy them on a large-scale strategic offensive, along lines roughly similar to those marked out by the AAFAC. Admiral King had eschewed an offensive for the entire length of the calendar year 1943. For 1944, Navy planners were preparing to deploy antisubmarine forces in a coordinated offensive with the object of destroying the enemy at sea, a policy which the AFFAC had developed from its inception. Signs were apparent by the middle of 1943, however, that indicated the Navy's intention to begin offensive action somewhat earlier. In April the Allied antisubmarine Survey Board urged employment of support groups, composed of aircraft carriers and destroyers to be given the primary mission of taking offensive action against submarines. It also urged that the "maximum effort" should be put into an offensive in the Bay of Biscay transit areas. All these offensive operations would, however, have to wait until sufficient convoy escort forces had been secured. A few days later Admiral Leahy, in a meeting of the JCS intimated that the only reason for the delay in offensive action was lack of forces. In May the question of an Allied offensive in the Bay of Biscay was again broached by the British Chiefs of Staff. By this time Admiral King offered only initial objections to diverting air units to that project. He maintained that an "irreducible minimum" of antisubmarine forces had to be maintained on the eastern coast of the United States because, while few submarines were currently in these waters, they could change their location more rapidly than aircraft. And he once again declared himself opposed to the mixing of forces in projects of this sort. As soon as it was demonstrated that an excess of VLR aircraft was located in Newfoundland, following the defeat in May of the U-boat packs in the North Atlantic, Admiral King solidly supported a plan for transferring as many as possible of those units to the United Kingdom for the purpose of participating in the Bay of Biscay offensive.

It is not surprising, then, that War Department observers looked on Navy plans relative to land-based aircraft with some apprehension, not unmixed with suspicion. As far as the AAFAC was concerned, it appeared that the Navy was intent either on duplicating its function within its own organization by the increased allocation of B-24's to be deployed on offensive operations, which would be patently wasteful, or on securing complete control of all antisubmarine aircraft, including those of the AAFAC, which would simply remove the danger of duplication to a much higher level and expand it on a much grander scale. The destiny of the AAFAC as a strategic air striking force then became inextricably tied up with the question of strategic air striking forces in general, a question which all but involved the separate existence of the Army Air Forces itself.

So the situation after the establishment of the Tenth Fleet remained extremely acute. Indeed it rapidly deteriorated. For the issues were now clearer, and it had become evident that control of the long-range antisubmarine air force could be disposed of in tow ways only: it could be given to the Army Air Forces, with or without the over-all operational supervision of the Navy, or it could be given completely to the naval authority. The AAFAC, acting merely as the AAF's contribution to the total antisubmarine air force, no longer occupied a tenable position. Logically speaking, there was plenty of middle ground. If, as General Larson himself maintained, the AAFAC were considered the "Strategic" antisubmarine air force and deployed exclusively as a long-range, mobile striking force, then the Navy air arm engaged in antisubmarine patrol could be left the job of close support of the Fleet in the peculiarly naval mission of protecting shipping, and thus become the "Tactical" antisubmarine air force – a division of command into two independent organizations, based on a natural division of function. But the force of circumstances now greatly outweighed the force of logic, and General Larson's conception of his Antisubmarine Command and its place in the military scheme of things bore little relation to the larger conflict of interests in which the Command had become involved.

Pending a final settlement with regard to the control of all air units engaged in antisubmarine warfare, there arose a grave danger that the air campaign itself might suffer. Fortunately, by June, the situation in the North Atlantic no longer threatened the very life line of US forces in the European Theater. But the situation in the Mediterranean depended on the still doubtful ability of ocean convoys to reach African and Mediterranean ports. It was to make safe the passage of those convoys that the Navy urged participation in the British offensive in the Bay of Biscay. The War Department, although well aware of the value of offensive action in this key area, was reluctant to commit US air units to the project until the question of their control could finally be made clear. The project was given War Department and AAF endorsement before any serious delay was experienced. The fact remained, however, that the AAFAC and those agencies having to do with its mission were handicapped by the impossibility of reconciling long term obligations with an immediately precarious status which necessitated planning on a short-term, emergency basis. This momentary hesitation on the part of the War Department helped to force the issue concerning the overall organization.

Final deliberations had already begun. On 10 June 1943, Rear Adm. McCain met with Generals Arnold and McHarney to draw up an agreement which would settle the question once and for all. From the documents available it is impossible to give a detailed account of the resulting discussions. Suffice it to say that an agreement was reached along the following lines:

(**turn this into a bullet or number list??**)

a.The Army is prepared to withdraw Army Air Forces from anti-submarine operation at such time as the Navy is ready to take over these duties completely.

b.Army anti-submarine airplanes would be continued in that service as long as the Navy has need for them.

c.Army anti-submarine B-24 airplanes would be turned over to the Navy in such numbers as they could be replaced by Navy combat B-24's.

d.The Navy is requested to submit a schedule on which the Army can turn over their planes to the Navy and draw Navy replacement B-24's.

e.The Fleet Air Wings which the Navy proposes to station along the Atlantic and Pacific Coasts will comprise only those types of aircraft whose primary functions are those of offshore patrol and reconnaissance and the protection of shipping.

f.It is primarily the responsibility of the Army to provide long-range bombing forces (currently called "strategic air forces") for operations from shore bases in defense of the Western Hemisphere and for appropriate operations in other theaters.

g.Long-range patrol planes assigned to Fleet Air Wings are for the primary purpose of conducting offshore patrol and reconnaissance and the protection of shipping, relieving Army long-range bombing forces from these duties.

h.Nothing in the foregoing sub-paragraphs is to be so interpreted as to limit or restrict a commander in the field, Army or Navy, in his use of all available aircraft as weapons of opportunity or necessity.

In effect the Arnold-McHarney-McCain agreement constituted a radical division of responsibility in the employment of long-range aircraft. In return for unquestioned control of all forces employed in protection of shipping, reconnaissance, and offshore patrol, the Navy would relinquish all claim to control of long-range striking forces operating from shore bases. The control of these so-called "strategic air forces" would remain, therefore, ineluctably an Army Air Forces responsibility. It was an agreement which affected issues far larger than that of the immediate fate of the AAFAC.

It was one thing to reach an agreement in committee and quite another to secure its approval by those more conservatively attached to the vested interest of their respective services. Neither Admiral King nor Secretary Stinson was willing to give up without a struggle. Admiral King accepted with alacrity the proposal that the Army hand over its antisubmarine responsibility to the Navy. It was, he said, a solution he was himself preparing to propose. He gave no indication, however, of turning over to the Army the quid pro quo by which the concession was to be obtained, apparently preferring to leave unsettled the Army's right to conduct other long-range striking operations by land-based planes.

To Secretary Stinson this failure of Admiral King's to endorse both halves of the Arnold-McHarney-McCain agreement seemed simply to guarantee continuation and infinitum of trouble between Army and Navy.

Furthermore, he was by no means convinced that the agreement itself promised any improvement in the war effort. He granted the wisdom of clarifying the over-all jurisdiction, provided the result was clear enough to eliminate friction between Army and Navy. But he seriously doubted if the antisubmarine campaign would profit by the elimination of an AAF organization staffed by young, air-minded men, trained in the use of long-range land-based bombers, and possessed of the initiative and inventiveness necessary to develop antisubmarine offensive measures to the utmost. The AAFAC had, he felt, embarked on a policy entirely foreign from anything the Navy had hitherto proposed. And it still possessed the equipment, personnel, and doctrine uniquely adapted to the purpose of destroying the submarines at sea.

Since reorganization was necessary, he had strongly supported the plan originally presented to the JCS by General Marshall, which provided an AAF commander for all land-based VLR planes, who would work under the general operational supervision of the Navy. The plan had an impressive precedent in the relation of the RAF Coastal Command to the Admiralty. To Secretary Stimson, it seemed the only reasonable way of insuring that a concerted offensive would be launched which would clear the Atlantic of submarines in advance of the "enormous stream of our troops which will have to cross that Ocean for the 1944 invasion." In his opinion the organization for antisubmarine warfare proposed by the Navy was deficient in the elements essential to success: namely, free initiative, exercised by men acquainted with modern methods, elasticity in the operation of these methods, and freedom from the limitations imposed by an organization based on coastal frontiers. If there views of Secretary Stinson's did less than justice to the resourcefulness of the US Navy, they full endorsed the potentialities existing in an AAF command for carrying an effective antisubmarine warfare.

In short, Secretary Stinson refused to approve the transfer of any antisubmarine activity to the Navy unless the latter were prepared to accept the entire Arnold-McHarney-McCain agreement, and he stated that he wished to be heard by the President on the subject should it reach the White House.

Faced with a possible impasse in a matter so close to the heart of the war effort, General Marshall issued what General Stratemeyer termed "one of the strongest and most important documents which has been signed by the Chief of Staff thus far during the war":

```
The question of responsibility for offensive operations against
submarines and that of responsibility for long-range air striking forces
are so closely related that a proper solution of one, in my opinion,
involves consideration of the other. The tentative
Arnold-McNarney-McCain agreement appeared to offer an acceptable
solution to both of those issues and solely on that basis I stated to
you in my memorandum of June 15 that your proposal to take over
anti-submarine air operations appeared to offer a practical solution to a
vexing problem which had adversely affected the efficiency of our
aerial war effort.
```

I should state here that in all of these Army and Navy air discussions I have tried very carefully to hold myself to a position from which I could consider the problems from a somewhat detached and I hope, purely logical basis. As I remarked in the meeting of the Joint chiefs of Staff the other day I feel that the present state of procedure between the Army and Navy is neither economical nor highly efficient and would inevitably meet with public condemnation were all the facts known. I have been hopeful that during the actual war effort we could manage our business in such a manner as to be spared the destructive effects of reorganizational procedure. But I am becoming more and more convinced that we must put our own house in order, and quickly, in order to justify our obligation to the country. I feel this very strongly because it is plain to me, however it may appear to others, that our present procedure is not at all what it should be.

Feeling as I do that the two questions involved are part and parcel of the same problem I believe that the Committee on Missions of the Army and Navy should be given both questions in their entirety for appropriate recommendation, or that we should formalize the entire Arnold-McNarney-McCain agreement. The latter procedure promises earlier, and I believe, more satisfactory results as it appears rather likely that the Committee may reach an impasse in the matter as the result of past strong prejudices and bitter discussions.

General Marshall made it clear that the Arnold-McNarney-McCain agreement did not establish a basis for the duplication of the long-range air striking force now in being in the Army. "Such duplication, if permitted, would be patently uneconomical and would result in an unavoidable drain on our resources." Meanwhile, he assured Admiral King that the AAFAC would continue to function, "insuring that no detriment to the war effort will occur as a result of any delay which may accrue while this matter is being properly settled."

On 9 July 1943, approximately 1 month after the Arnold-McNarney-McCain committee convened, its agreement was accepted by both War and

Navy Departments. A schedule was subsequently established whereby 77 Army antisubmarine-equipped B-24's would be transferred with related equipment to the Navy, in return for an equal number of combat-equipped B-24's from Navy allocations. The transfer was to take place gradually from the latter part of July to the end of September. Some difficulty arose over the relief of the squadrons on duty in the United Kingdom and in Northwest Africa. Finally it was decided to keep them in their current duty status until such time as they could be relieved by similarly equipped Navy squadrons. On 6 October 1943, Bombardment Branch, Operations, Commitments, and Requirements, was able to report that the 77 planes in the original agreement had been transferred. In October, also, the Navy Liberators arrived at Dunkeswell, Devonshire, to relieve the 479th Group. By the middle of November, the 480th Group had been relieved and was on its way back to Langley Field from Northwest Africa.

The AAFAC officially passed out of the picture before the complicated mechanism of transfer could be completed. By an order, dated 31 August, from Headquarters, EDC and First Air Force, its headquarters was re-designated Headquarters, I Bomber Command, and assigned to the First Air Force, effective 24 August 1943. The AAFAC wings, the 25th and 26th, were inactivated and their personnel, together with all excess personnel left over from the earlier expansion made necessary by the increase in antisubmarine activity, were made available to AC/AS, Personnel for reassignment. The domestic squadrons, 17 of the 25 separate squadrons of the command, were re-designated as heavy bombardment units and assigned to the Second Air Force. The 18th Squadron, which had operated as an OUT at Langley Field, was assigned to the 1st Sea-Search Attack Group of the First Air Force for the purpose of conducting replacement crew training on radar equipment. The 23d Squadron continued temporarily to serve as a special task unit, on special duty with the Navy in the Caribbean for the purpose of experimenting with 75mx, armament in B-25 aircraft, after which it went, with the bulk of the other squadrons, to the Second Air Force. The 479th Group, with four squadrons stationed in the United Kingdom, was inactivated and its personnel and equipment)the latter not a part of the 77-plane agreement) assigned to the Eighth Air Force, its personnel to be used as a nucleus in forming a pathfinder group. Similarly, the 450th Group returned intact to the United States, whereupon the bulk of its personnel was assigned to the Second Air Force, a few of the officers remaining on duty with Headquarters, AAF. Its aircraft were made available for use in the American and Pacific theaters. Both the 479th and the 480th Groups continued operations until the latter part of October 1943.

As this slow process neared completion, and the Army Air Forces prepared to bow finally from the stage of antisubmarine operations, the work of its deceased Antisubmarine Command became the subject of several laudatory statements, in which Admirals King and Andrews joined with General Arnold and others, who were in like position to know whereof they spoke, in pronouncing it a job well done.

If there is one fact which stands out above another in this story of the policies and concept surrounding the Army Air Forces' participation in the antisubmarine campaign, it is that the fate of the AAFAC depended not at all on its doctrine of antisubmarine warfare or on its ability to fulfill the requirements of it mission. Throughout most of the story a sharp cleavage in strategic doctrine had emphasized a cleavage already existing between the services jointly engaged in the work. And there were those who, like Secretary Stinson and General Larson, maintained to the end the value of the Army doctrine and the unique ability of Army air officers to implement it. But, although committed to an organization which scarcely allowed the flexibility considered in air circles essential to the highest efficiency in antisubmarine warfare, and possessed of less adequate experience in the operation of land-based aviation than the AAF, the Navy was ready in the summer of 1943 to project an offensive which the AAFAC had preached since its previous incarnation as the I Bomber Command. There doubtless still existed a difference of opinion relative to the priority to be attached to offensive operations. To the Navy, convoy escort probably still ranked above killer tactics. Nevertheless, the Navy was prepared to throw everything possible into an effort to destroy the U-boats at sea as soon as the minimum requirements for defense had been met. And, thanks to the substantial defeat of the U-boats during May, June, and July, these requirements could be met at an earlier date than naval plans appear initially to have anticipated.

The question at issue therefore was not strategic or even tactical, but rather the larger one of jurisdiction over long-range, land-based air striking forces. With reference to this more comprehensive problem, control of the AAFAC constituted little more than a test case. But the importance of a test case is determined by the importance of the issue being tested, and the case of the AAFAC becomes consequently one of the most significant arising in the US armed forces during the present war.

3

THE BATTLE OF THE ATLANTIC

It was a large and already crowded stage onto which the AAF Antisubmarine Command stepped in October 1943. The Battle of the Atlantic had not yet reached its peak of intensity, nor had any decisive blows been struck, but several phases of the conflict had already come and gone and several agencies were engaged in an effort to defeat the Nazi raiders. At first, in 1939 and 1940, the U-boats had operated with immunity close to the British Isles and the coast of Europe. The British had made every effort to counter the submarine blockade and had, in fact, cleared the English Channel and North Sea waters with fair success. As yet, however, aircraft were used only to a limited extent, and long-range air patrols were unheard of. The summer of 1941 saw a marked increase in the use of air power, nearly one-third of the damaging attacks being credited to them. The result was that the U-boats moved farther afield, scattering their attacks as far west as 49 degrees, and as far south as Africa. Effective air patrol remained relatively short-ranged, leaving the whole central ocean a free hunting ground for the enemy.

The next phase of the battle began upon the entry of the United States into the war. The resulting depredations off the US Atlantic coastline General Marshall felt jeopardized the entire war effort. By the middle of June 1942, he reported that 17 of the 74 ships allocated to the Army for July had already been sunk, 32 per cent of the bauxite fleet, and 20 per cent of the Puerto Rican fleet had been lost, and tanker sinking's had amounted to 3.5 per cent per month of the tonnage in use.

By the fall of that year an entirely new act in the drama was begun. The enemy had gradually withdrawn from the Eastern and Gulf Sea Frontiers, partly because of the increased opposition he encountered in American waters and partly because the Allied invasion of North Africa made it essential for the U-boat fleet to turn from its aggressive campaign against shipping in general in order to concentrate defensively against the invasion convoys. The U-boat fleet continued, however, to operate actively and effectively in areas, such as the waters off Trinidad, where the traffic was relatively large and the antisubmarine measures relatively weak.

By the time the AAF Antisubmarine Command was activated, two things had become clear about the submarine war. One was that the Germans would, if at all possible, avoid areas provided with adequate antisubmarine forces. The other was that the most flexible and among the most powerful of these forces consisted of long-range bombardment aircraft, specially equipped and manned for the purpose of hunting and killing submarines. Though dictated primarily by the necessity of destroying as much Allied shipping as possible and preventing the Allies from implementing any logistical plan of major importance, German strategy in the Atlantic always remained sensitive to the state of Allied antisubmarine forces, especially air forces. Throughout the antisubmarine war, wherever adequate air cover was provided the submarine withdrew, if tactically possible. In the region of the British Isles, when the same submarine was sighted an average of six times a month it left the area, and when sighted an average of three times a month in American coastal waters it left them. As for the relative effectiveness of aircraft compared to surface vessels, Dr. Bowles, in March 1943, estimated aircraft to be about 10 times as effective in finding submarines as surface craft and at least as effective in killing them.

The U-boat fleet, although strategically on the defensive, had still ample opportunity to operate effectively. The EAF Coastal Command and the Royal Navy had made the British waters unprofitable for it, and had seriously interfered with its free access to the submarine bases on the European coast. The AAF and US Navy had cleared American waters as far south as the Caribbean. But the convoy routes, especially those in the North Atlantic, which bore the weight of Allied strategic supplies, remained relatively unprotected. For air cover, in the absence of adequate very-long-range equipment, could only protect an area a few hundred miles offshore. This left a large gap in mid-ocean without cover, and as yet the Allies did not have enough strength in carrier escort vessels to provide air cover for this area. Moreover, the Atlantic U-boat fleet was believed to be increasing rather than otherwise. Probably not more than 15 to 22 enemy submarines were operating in the Atlantic at the beginning of 1942. At the end of the year this force had risen to about 108, and the Germans were believed to be producing submarines at the rate of between 20 and 25 per month.

After a highly successful month in November 1942, the Germans spent a relatively unprofitable winter. Their strategy was apparently to throw out mid-ocean screens in a primarily defensive plan to destroy Allied convoys. It may have been owing to this thinly deployed screen of submarines, extending from 55 degrees north latitude to slightly south of the equator and through which convoys could frequently pass without detection, that few merchant vessels were lost that winter. It may also have been true that the Germans were conserving their forces for a total spring offensive. At any rate, toward the end of February and during the early days of March 1943, it became evident that they were adopting a new strategy involving a concentration of U-boats along the North Atlantic convoy routes. Concurrently with this shifting of forces, the enemy also planned to hold large forces of Allied antisubmarine aircraft and escort vessels in widely scattered control areas. This they could do without too much expenditure of submarines simply by sending small groups into the Eastern, Gulf, and Caribbean Sea Frontiers and the Brazilian, Freetown, and Mozambique areas.

The disposition of enemy forces in the North Atlantic followed a general pattern somewhat as follows. Two roughly parallel screens running in a northwesterly direction were thrown across the convoy routes in such a way as to make contact with both eastbound and westbound convoys. As soon as convoys were attacked, the two lines would break formation and gather around the convoy, resuming the parallel screen formation when all feasible measures had been taken to harass the Allied ships. This strategy worked well and accounted for most of the sinking sin the Atlantic, which rose once again to a dangerous total in March. In that month, too, the Allied nations immediately concerned in the Battle of the Atlantic took action to close the gap in their North Atlantic defenses. The Atlantic Convoy Conference met, and plans were laid to employ effective long-range air forces in Newfoundland, Greenland, and Iceland.

The Battle of the North Atlantic reached its climax in early May with the attack on a convoy known as ONS-5. Frustrated by increasingly effective surface escort and air patrol, the Germans threw a large force of submarines into a running battle in a reckless attempt to retrieve some kind of victory from their dwindling spring offensive. So reckless was their attack that they lost heavily, and were forced to admit the failure of their attempt to close off the North Atlantic routes. In addition to an increasing number of air attacks of better quality than ever before, the Germans owed their defeat to the introduction by the Allies of aircraft carriers which were able to provide air coverage in any part of the ocean. Planned aerial escort of convoys by carrier-based aircraft had been inaugurated in March.

By early July the enemy had almost abandoned the North Atlantic and the vital war convoys could proceed unmolested. The estimated average daily density of U-boats in the area declined from 58 in May to 16 in June and only 5 in July. Ship losses decreased correspondingly from a peak of 38 in March to 14 in May and none in July, despite the fact that nearly 1700 ship crossings were accomplished in June and July.

Meanwhile, since October 1943, AAF bombers of the Eighth Air Force had joined EAF forces in bombing attacks on German submarine bases, construction yards, and parts plants. This action did little to reduce the number of U-boats at sea nor did it do as much as had been expected to retard the output of submarines, the estimated number of completions by early 1944 having been reduced by not more than 20. Meanwhile, also, the RAF, with the brief help of two AAF Antisubmarine Command squadrons, was pressing an offensive campaign in the Bay of Biscay transit area. And both aircraft and surface forces engaged in the antisubmarine war were gradually increasing in effectiveness, as a result of improved weapons and devices, and the increasing experience of their crews.

It was clear, then, that the Allies, though hampered by lack of unified command, were successfully employing four main methods in their counterattack against the U-boats. First, they were maintaining defensive patrols in coastal areas to hamper and restrict enemy operations. Secondly, they were employing defensive convoy escort and offensive sweeps around convoys in order to prevent the submarine packs from closing in for the attack. Thirdly, offensive bombing missions were being pressed against U-boat bases and building yards. Finally, screens of surface craft and aircraft were being thrown in a continuous offensive action across areas in which U-boats were forced to concentrate.

A corollary to the increasingly effective antisubmarine campaign may be found in the increasing tendency of the U-boats to fight back. Prior to the spring of 1943, the standard practice on the part of U-boat commanders was to employ a passive defense against air attack and simply to dive on the approach of an enemy plane. If too many planes were encountered, however, a new problem arose. The submarine could not remain submerged indefinitely nor could it make the speed necessary for successful attacks while under water. The decision to employ an active defense came therefore as an admission of the effectiveness of air patrol. It also, of course, gave the attacking aircraft a substantial target for its depth bombs. During July of 1943 these defensive tactics, apparently adopted throughout the U-boat fleet, served to intensify the speed of the submarine war.

Especially vigorous was the action in the eastern Atlantic. It had been anticipated that the enemy, driven from the North Atlantic convoy routes, would move his forces south to the convoy routes between the United Staten and the Mediterranean. The latter lanes were not only carrying a substantial and steadily increasing amount of vital traffic in support of the North African and Sicilian campaigns, but, owing to lack of antisubmarine bases in the Azores, much of the route was out of range of land-based aircraft. This anticipation proved entirely correct, for the German formed heavy U-boat concentrations south and southwest of the Azores. These submarines enjoyed surprisingly little success. Several factors may have reduced the effectiveness of their groups. Convoys could be widely dispersed in the wide expanse of the mid-Atlantic; heavy escort was provided, especially for the high-speed troop convoys; and the small aircraft carriers operated effectively in this area.

Certainly another factor was the action of British and AAF Antisubmarine Command aircraft in the Bay of Biscay transit area and in the approaches to Gibraltar. AAF Antisubmarine Command squadrons were sent in July to reinforce the British offensive in the Bay of Biscay and long-range patrol of the approaches to Gibraltar had been increased in March by the transfer to Northwest Africa of two AAF Antisubmarine Command squadrons from the United Kingdom. In June and July these areas saw some of the sharpest action of the Atlantic war in operations which frustrated any further attempt on the part of the enemy to reorganize a concentrated offensive. During these operations, the Germans threw large forces of medium and heavy aircraft into defensive attacks on antisubmarine aircraft.

September saw a sadly reduced, if still potentially dangerous, submarine fleet being employed by the Germans in the Atlantic. The Germans had deployed an average force of about 103 U-boats in the Atlantic during the first five months of 1943. In contrast to these figures, probably not more than 50 were operating in the Atlantic by early September. Moreover, the U-boats were now being manned by relatively inexperienced crews, since probably 7000 trained crew members and officers had been lost in the submarines, estimated at upwards of 150, either sunk or probably sunk during the previous 8 months. Most encouraging of all was the fact that from July to September 1943 only one-half of 1 per cent of US supplies shipped in the Atlantic were lost through submarine attack.

In accomplishing this great change in U-boat warfare, which until the end of 1942 had run entirely in favor of the enemy, aircraft played a major role. By July 1943, aircraft were making 60 to 70 per cent of all attacks on U-boats and by the end of the year it was estimated that about 70 per cent of the submarines being sunk were lost to aircraft, either land-based or carrier-based. The answer to the U-boat menace had been found to an overwhelming degree in action at sea, and by air attack in particular.

This, in rough outline, was the pattern of events in which the AAF Antisubmarine Command found a not inconspicuous place.

4

OPERATIONS IN THE EASTERN ATLANTIC

The Bay of Biscay. The summer of 1943 had left the Eastern and Gulf Sea Frontiers almost free from the undersurface raiders. While the bulk of the Antisubmarine Command's operational squadrons were engaged in defensive convoy coverage or in the patrol of these uninfected waters, a few units were being allowed to test the command's doctrine of the strategic offensive, and to hunt the U-boats where they abounded, either in their home waters or where they were forced by strategic necessity to be. In November 1942, one squadron of B-24's, equipped with SGR-517C radar, was sent to England. In January another joined it. During the course of its career, the command sent, in all, six VLR squadrons to operate in the Eastern Atlantic. These units, ultimately organized into the 479th and 480th Antisubmarine Groups, contributed the most significant chapter in the AAFAC operational history.

Probably the most interesting aspect of their eastern Atlantic operations was the participation by the American squadrons in the Bay of Biscay offensive being conducted almost continuously by the British Coastal Command during the period covered by this study. Their participation was of brief duration, but the results were extremely instructive to students of antisubmarine warfare and destructive to the enemy.

The "Bay offensive" had, by 1943, become the pivotal point for the entire British antisubmarine effort. The strategic theory behind it was very logical. It was well known that most of the U-boats operating in the Atlantic, estimated at upwards of 100, were based on ports on the western coast of France. In order to leave these parts for operations against Atlantic shipping and to return for necessary periodic repair and convincing, practically the entire German submarine fleet had to pass through the Bay of Biscay, thus producing a constantly high concentration in the Bay and its approaches. Moreover, in crossing this transit area, the U-boats were obliged to spend an appreciable portion of their time on the surface in order to recharge their batteries. It soon occurred to the Coastal Command that the judicious use of a moderate air force in this area would be enough eventually to cripple the U-boat offensive.

Throughout the first 6 months of 1942 the Coastal Command flew a small but steadily increasing number of hours in the Biscay transit area. During the next year, the flying effort in that area was maintained at a relatively high level, averaging between 3000 and 4000 hours per month. The chief problems to be overcome were lack of very-long-range aircraft capable of covering the entire transit area from English bases, lack of a "balanced" antisubmarine force capable of attacking both by day and night, thus making it just as dangerous for U-boats to surface by night as by day, and lack radar equipment of a kind the Germans could not detect. Early in 1943 a plan was being drawn up, based on comprehensive theoretical studies, calling for an increased and better-balanced flying effort in the Bay of Biscay. An area was determined in the approaches to the Bay, of much size that every U-boat in transit must surface at least once to recharge its batteries. The expected density of surfaced U-boats in the area was then calculated. It was estimated that a certain number of sorties by specially equipped planes would be required, by day and night, to insure that every submarine in transit would be subjected to attack. It was planned to make extensive use of Mark III radar, which the Germans were apparently unable to detect, in conjunction with the Leigh searchlight in order to make night operations effective. It was claimed that a force of 260 suitably equipped aircraft could account for about 25 U-boats killed and 34 damaged per month. Even a force of about 40 long-range aircraft was considered enough to make the enemy abandon the Bay ports, because the u-boats in transit had no retreat from a well-equipped air force. And to abandon the Bay ports would mean defeat in the Atlantic, for the Germans could not use Norwegian ports without risking a similarly concentrated offensive in a similar transit area off Scotland and Ireland.

The question had arisen whether this air force would be used to better advantage in a defensive-offensive campaign in the area where the U-boats actually operated. But it was decided that, inasmuch as the Bay offensive, if pressed constantly, would lead to a breaking point, and therefore to total defeat of the U-boats in the Atlantic, it should have priority over the necessarily defensive campaign against the enemy in his operational area. In the open sea the U-boat could choose its time and place, surface or submerge, more nearly at will than was possible in the vital transit area. On the ground of morale alone it was believed the Bay offensive could do irreparable damage to the U-boat fleet.

This was the strategic situation into which the 1st and 2d AAF Antisubmarine Squadrons were projected in February of 1943. They had been dispatched to the United Kingdom originally for the purpose of training in Coastal Command methods. When thoroughly indoctrinated, they were to proceed to North Africa for action with the Twelfth Air Force. While in England, however, plans were altered somewhat. The British were at this point (early 1943) in serious need of long-range antisubmarine aircraft. Though their operations in the Bay had been successful, it was believed that the U-boats were able to remain submerged long enough, with possible brief night surfacing, to carry them beyond the outer limit of the British medium-range planes. It was therefore decided to use the two American squadrons of B-24's to supplement the few available long-range British aircraft in a thorough patrol of the outer area, far to the west. The medium-range equipment would then be concentrated in the inner area. These areas were called Outer and Inner Gondola, respectively. In view of the then chronic shortage of aircraft, the sustained effort of this Gondola operation was planned to continue for only 9 days, and was dated to coincide with an estimated inrush of U-boats coming away from two coveys battles then in full conflict. The period was actually 6 to 15 February 1943. The results confirmed the wisdom of the plan. Fourteen sightings resulted in nine attacks in Outer Gondola. Only four sightings and one attack came from the inner area. Of the enemy contacts made in the outer area, 90 per cent were by the US aircraft. Thus, Air Marshal Slessor, Air-Officer-Commanding-in-Chief, wrote, some months later, "The two US squadrons ... played the major part and incidentally blooded themselves in most successfully in the Anti-U/Boat War on this side of the Atlantic.

This is all somewhat ahead of the story. And the Gondola offensive is really only part of the story. It was no single task to transplant two American squadrons and train them under foreign conditions to such a point that they could turn in a record such as that outlined above. Many US bombardment squadrons had preceded them to England and as components of the Eighth Air Force had become successfully operational. But they had from the beginning formed part of a well-organized and sizeable American force, and had pioneered in an entirely different type of warfare from that to which the 1st and 2d Antisubmarine Squadrons were committed. The latter units, in fact, found the way but poorly prepared for them in the United Kingdom.

To begin with, on its arrived at St. Eval on 7 November 1942, the advance units of the 1st Antisubmarine Squadron found that no one know anything of the plans for it. The decision to send it and the 2d Antisubmarine Squadron had been made in haste and in great secrecy, and it took the commanding officer, Lt. Col. Jack Roberts, some time to find out where his unit should operate and under whose control. After a series of conversations with the Commanding General of the Eighth Air Force, it was finally settled that the squadron should be attached to the VIII Bomber Command for supply and administration, and that it should remain at St. Eval under the operational control of the EAF Coastal Command. When the 2d Antisubmarine Squadron arrived in January 1943, it was stationed at the same field and placed under the same administrative control. On 15 January 1943 the two squadrons were combined in the 1st Antisubmarine Group (Prov.), under the command of Colonel Roberts, working as a detached unit of the 25th Antisubmarine Wing of the AAF Antisubmarine Command.

It had been understood prior to departure from the United States that maintenance for aircraft would be provided immediately after arrival. Actually, there were no adequate facilities or personnel for this purpose. The VIII Bomber Command quickly detached 85 mechanics, ordnance men, armament specialists, and guards, but the men were not experienced in B-2d aircraft at that time, and they joined the group reluctantly since it meant leaving their own promotion lists. It proved to be a considerable problem to weld these men into an efficient maintenance team, but one that was fortunately soon solved.

St. Eval was already overcrowded with squadrons of the Coastal Command. No hangar space was available for maintenance. The result was that all such work had to be done during the limited number of daylight hours in the open, the mechanics unprotected from the raw weather of a British winter. Nearly 50 per cent of the personnel immediately contracted heavy bronchial colds, a situation which presented a real problem to the flight surgeon who lacked even the simplest medicines. Furthermore, there were no quarters available for the officers and men at the station, so it was necessary to scatter them at considerable distances from the field. For quite a while, too, the American units had to eat British rations, since no separate mess facilities had been provided.

St. Eval was far removed from any established Services of Supply or Air Service Command supply depots, finance offices, or Army post offices, nor had any adequate communications or supply channels been set up to reach it. As a result, the nearest depots were at first a difficult day's drive away. Later, a newly established depot was located that could be reached by a 5-hour drive.

In addition to these initial difficulties, there were several serious administrative and operational problems which could scarcely have been solved until the units were in the theater. The squadrons had been sent to England with no idea of prolonged operations in that area. They, therefore, found themselves short of personnel, a situation which was not improved by generally prevalent illness. Officer personnel was especially overtaxed. Moreover, since the group was at that time provisional, the commanding officer found himself without adequate authority in some respects. For example, he could neither promote deserving personnel nor demote a few recalcitrant individuals – in either case a condition detrimental to group morale. The squadrons were immediately faced with innumerable problems in learning British control methods, navigational aids, communications, and other procedures. Even some British customs provided minor but troublesome prob-

lems. British military custom, for instance, draws a sharp line of demarca-
tion among enlisted men between sergeants and those of lower rank, and
provides each group with its own housing and recreational facilities. The
American crews had to be similarly divided although such division was con-
trary to US Army custom.

Some difficulty arose over the nature of the "operational control" to be
exercised by the Coastal Command. As in the case of the U.S. Navy's control, the term had not been clearly defined. Questions at once arose. Did
operational control mean that missions could be ordered if weather conditions were, in the opinion of the group commander, too hazardous? Would
he have a voice in determining assignments? There and similar questions
carried serious potentialities which could easily have wreaked current and
future cooperation between Allied commands. Officers of the group had,
however, nothing but praise for the cooperation they received from the
RAF Coastal Command. That organization gave freely of its long experience in antisubmarine warfare, a contribution which proved invaluable in
guiding and training the novice squadrons. It left to the group commander
final decision on all assignments as well as on all questions of recall or diversion of missions, whether owing to weather or enemy activity. The Army
Air Forces Controller, who worked directly with the British Controller, had
the full privilege of handling all control of American aircraft if in his judgment intervention was advisable. British radio communications proved to
be excellent and the British control officers soon gained the complete confidence of all flying personnel. The British spared no effort in guiding aircraft
to safe bases, regardless of risks involved, and fields were always fully lighted
for landings despite the constant and often immediate threat of attack from
enemy aircraft operating from bases only 100 miles distant.

The 1st Antisubmarine Squadron flew its first mission in European
waters on 16 November 1943, just 9 days after its arrived in the United
Kingdom. Operations continued rather slowly for a while, since at first only
three planes were available. Additional aircraft became operational during
the following 90 days. Exactly 2 months later, on 17 January 1943, the 2d
Antisubmarine Squadron flew its first mission. These small initial operations provided invaluable experience, for they demonstrated the operational
problems that were to face all US squadrons in European areas, and they

served as laboratory tests that proved the amount and type of additional training needed for newly arrived units.

The job of training to meet the conditions of operation in the eastern Atlantic, and under the control of the British, was a large one. Much instruction had to be given in the use of British depth bombs, in British methods of diverting aircraft to alternate fields when weather proved suddenly adverse, and in British control and radio procedures which differed substantially from American. Recognition of enemy and friendly aircraft had to be exact in an area covered by enemy as well as by friendly patrols. Enemy capabilities, tactics, and methods of combat had to be learned. Extra training in navigation was especially important since many of the navigational aids to which US navigators were accustomed, such as radio beams, could not be used in the ETO; and even a small navigational error in returning from a 2000-mile sea mission might put the aircraft over enemy territory.

As for equipment, the new SCR-517C radar proved the principal problem. The aircraft of the squadrons had been equipped with this latest device immediately prior to leaving the United Stat4es. A supply of spare parts was lost en route, the equipment had not been "shaken down" before departure, the radar operators in the organization had not been trained in its use, and experienced mechanics could not be found in the United Kingdom. Once these initial difficulties had been surmounted, the radar sets proved their worth accounting for many sightings that probably could not have been made with British equipment. The B-24 aircraft themselves gave very little trouble. The only serious difficulty arose in adapting them to carry 10 to 12 of the British Torpex 250-pound depth bombs without shifting forward the center of gravity of the airplane.

The chain of command in the Coastal Command was similar to that in the AAF Antisubmarine Command. The 1st Provisional Group operated under the Station Commander, St. Eval, who received his orders from Headquarters, 19 Group, RAF, which corresponded to the wing organization in the AAF Antisubmarine Command. The squadrons reported daily to the Station Controller the number of planes and crews available for missions the following day. The Controller then assigned take-off times. Crews reported for briefing 2 hours prior to scheduled takeoff and received lunches, pyrotechnics, and all other equipment and information relative to the mission. Operational missions generally were of 11 to 14 hours' duration in order to make full use of the long-range potentialities of the B-24. Such long missions, searching far out over the ocean, proved exceedingly fatiguing to the combat crews, especially when executed under adverse weather conditions. When it is considered that these squadrons arrived in the United Kingdom at the beginning of the worst months normally experienced in a country not noted for its fine winter climate, it can readily be seen that the long-distance patrols were only for tough and young men. Missions at first were planned every third day, but it was found that, in the interests of the mental and physical health of the men, 3 days would have to elapse between missions.

The following table indicates the extent of operations of the group from the United Kingdom:

Month	Missions	Hrs. Flown	U-boat Sightings	Attacks
Nov. 1942	9	77	0	0
Dec. 1942	30	231	2	2
Jan. 1943	58	490	1	0
Feb. 1943	111	1052	15	8
Mar. 1-5, 1943	10	116	2	1
	218	1966	20	11

In view of the fact that few aircraft were available during November and December 1942, and that the 2d Antisubmarine Squadron did not fly its first operational mission until 16 January 1943, the record of nearly 2000 hours of operational flying during the months of worst British weather is highly satisfactory. The record of sightings and attacks is also good. On the average, 1 sighting was made for every 93.3 hours of flying time, and 1 attack for each 177.8 hours of flight, a record far more satisfying than that being achieved during the same period on the US Atlantic coast where the scarcity of U-boats necessitated many thousands of hours of flying for each sighting. Most striking of all, however, are the figures for the Gondola campaign in early February. This action proved to be the climax of the operations of the 1st Provisional Group (later the 480th Group) during its stay in the United Kingdom.

On 20 occasions, aircraft of the group, while operating from the United Kingdom, sighted enemy U-boats. In 11 instances attacks followed. In the remaining 9, the U-boat had been submerged so long before the arrival of the attacking aircraft that no depth bombs were released, a procedure quite in accordance with instructions. In these early months of operation a great deal of difficulty was experienced in adjusting release mechanisms to function properly with the British type of depth bomb. In 3 out of 11 attacks made, the depth bombs "hung up" and so frustrated what might otherwise have been excellent attacks. Of the 3 attacks not thwarted by mechanical failure, the assessed results were:

1 probably sunk
1 so severely damaged that it probably failed to reach port
1 severely damaged
3 insufficient evidence of damage
2 no damage

The aircraft of the group did not conduct these early operations unopposed. For many months Allied aircraft had been free to fly over the Bay without opposition from enemy planes, but, as the Allied air patrols increased and crossing the Bay became correspondingly more difficult, the enemy began to put medium-range twin-engine fighters over the area in increasing numbers. This tendency was becoming apparent during the period when the 480th Group operated from the United Kingdom. Some months later, the 476th Group encountered much greater opposition from the JU-88's. During the winter months, aircraft of the 480th Group engaged enemy planes on four occasions. As a result, two JU-88's were at least damaged and quite possibly destroyed. They were last seen losing altitude rapidly and smoking heavily. On another occasion one of the group was known to have engaged in aerial combat but failed to return to its base or render any report by radio. Two other aircraft failed to return to their base, but no indication remains as to the cause of their loss.

The successful operations of the 480th Antisubmarine Group from St. Eval were not accomplished without cost in lives and aircraft. In all, 65 officers and men lost their lives, and 7 B-24's were destroyed. Of the latter, 2 were lost in crossing the Atlantic to England, 2 failed to return from a mission, their fate unknown, 2 crashed, and the seventh was doubtless destroyed in aerial combat.

In March 1943 the 480th Group was ordered to Port Lyautey, French Morocco, to engage in antisubmarine patrol of the vital approaches to the TORCH area. The final missions from the United Kingdom were flown on 5 March. In 6 weeks of full operations and during the preceding 2 months of limited operations, the 480th Group had made a very solid contribution to the antisubmarine effort in the eastern Atlantic. Of the 49 sightings and 25 attacks made during the critical month of February by all units operating on antisubmarine duty from the United Kingdom and Iceland, the 1st and 3d Antisubmarine Squadrons alone accounted for 15 sightings and 5 completed attacks. Even more important was the pioneering work done in foreign operations, a contribution which led to the solution of many troublesome administrative and technical problems. Their withdrawal was noted by the British Coastal Command "with keen regret."

The campaign of early February in the Gondola area had demonstrated the feasibility of a sustained and concentrated air offensive in the Bay of Biscay. After the departure of the 4805h Antisubmarine Group, the Coastal Command continued to hit the U-boats in transit as heavily as its resources would permit. The British also agitated with increasing insistence for an Allied offensive, launched on an unprecedented scale, in the Bay area. In March it was proposed by the British that a combined British and American contribution of 180 additional VLR, ASV-equipped aircraft and crews be organized, to be added to the force of 100 aircraft then said to be devoted by the Coastal Command to the Bay patrol. This force would constitute the tactical elements of a specially staffed British and American organization to be assigned the specific mission of offensive air operations in the approaches to the Bay of Biscay during the period May to August, inclusive. The plan, involving as it did the creation of a distinct task force, separate in organization, did not coincide with AAF plans which conceived the May project as but one aspect of a single war task of much broader scope, namely, the protection of the Atlantic lines of communication against submarine attack. Furthermore, it was pretty obvious that any implementing of the Bay of Biscay plan would have to be done by the AAF at the expense of EFO heavy-bombing operations, for the US Navy was not planning to do more than add 45 planes to those already engaged in North Atlantic anti-submarine activity. The AAF was both unwilling to compromise its current commitments of heavy bombers and crews to the Eighth Air Force and reluctant to incur further commitments with regard to the Atlantic antisub-marine campaign until it could be finally determined what organization would ultimately be responsible for US air operations against submarines in the Atlantic. The British authorities felt strongly that the Bay offensive would do more than any other single factor to end the "present unsatisfac-tory progress in the Battle of the Atlantic." And time, in this instance, was at a premium: 3 to 6 months later, the Germans might be shifting their efforts to Norway, thereby necessitating an entirely new project, and one less fea-sible than that proposed in the Bay of Biscay.

Support for this view came from an unexpected source. The US Navy, which had been hitherto officially against the use of antisubmarine forces in a purely offensive campaign, came, in June 1943, to favor the plan and urge its adoption. Admiral King, early in June, had suggested that two Army VLR squadrons be sent from Newfoundland to the United Kingdom to partici-pate in the Bay of Biscay project. There were, he pointed out, more VLS air-craft in the Newfoundland area than were set up as a minimum requirement for that area by the Atlantic Convoy Conference (ACC 3). Finally, in the latter part of June, the 4th and 19th Antisubmarine Squadrons were ordered from Newfoundland to duty in the United Kingdom. Those units became the backbone of the 479th Antisubmarine Group, activated in England in July 1943.

Meanwhile, the British had gone ahead with plans of their own for a con-centrated offensive in the Bay and its approaches. The losses, which had been inflicted on the U-boats in May, forced the German command to with-draw their fleet from the North Atlantic convoy route and to operate against independent shipping in scattered areas. This shift in enemy strategy forced the British to redouble their efforts in the Bay transit area, for there alone could the enemy be found with any degree of certainty. Accordingly, it was decided in early June to concentrate in the Bay offensive all available aircraft not required for close escort of convoys, and to reinforce these by surface support groups withdrawn from the convoy routes. The resulting joint anti-submarine striking forces were deployed in tow new antisubmarine areas in the Bay known as "Musketry" and "Scaslug." Reinforcement of the patrol of these areas, especially in their southern reaches, came from the Allied forces in the Moroccan Sea Frontier and at Gibraltar. The newly intensified offensive met with early success. The enemy attempted to counter it by sending their submarines through the bay in close groups of two, three, sometimes even five. This practice, while it concentrated a formidable screen of antiaircraft fire against individual patrolling planes, prevented a tempting target for a well-balanced antisubmarine force. On 30 July a whole group of three U-boats was sunk in a combined air and surface action.

The 479th Group began its work in the United Kingdom with a double advantage in its favor. Not only had the project been less hastily organized than that of the 450th, but it profited from the pioneering work done in the field by the older unit. Upon the arrival of its flight echelon at St. Eval (the first 13 airplanes landed there on 30 June, the remaining 11 on 7 July), the group was placed under the Eighth Air Force for administration and supply and under the 19 Group, RAF Coastal Command, for operational control. It was decided not to keep it at St. Eval but to turn over to its use a new field at Dunkeswell, Devonshire. At this field the men of the 479th enjoyed the advantage of a relatively separate establishment, under the control of Col. Howard Noore, commanding officer of the group, with Group Captain Kidd of the Coastal Command exercising only a general supervision. The 87th Service Squadron, the 1813th Ordnance Service and Maintenance Company, the 1177th Military Police Company, and the 444th Quartermaster Platoon arrived in England with the group's ground echelon and were attached to it at Dunkeswell. It is not surprising, then, that the 479th escaped some of the more vexing administrative and logistical problems which faced the 480th on its arrival. The men of the 479th even received American rations at this new station. The incomplete state of construction at Dunkeswell did, it is true, impose some discomfort on the new occupants. Nevertheless, the group at once settled down to training under the novel conditions of operations in the United Kingdom. The problems met in this regard were much the same as those encountered by the 480th. On 13 July aircraft of the 479th Group flew their first operational missions.

Not long afterward (29 July) Air Marshal Slessor spoke of the "most welcome reinforcement" provided by the two squadrons of the group for the

"Muskestry" area where the hunting had been quite good this month. The 479th had indeed taken an active part in the Muskestry campaign. During the nineteen days aircraft of the 4th and 19th squadrons sighted 13 submarines and attacked 7 of them. Of those attacked, 3 were known to have been sunk, two with the aid of RAF aircraft patrolling in the vicinity. Enemy tactics thereafter changed. The U-boats abandoned the policy of staying on the surface and fighting the attacking aircraft and henceforth made every effort to avoid surfacing during daylight hours. After a successful attack on 2 August only 1 additional sighting occurred during the entire remaining period of operation, to 31 August; and even this sighting did not result in a successful attack.

Most of the attacks (six out of eight) made by the 479th Group were made in the face of determined countermeasures on the part of the U-boat crews. In a desperate attempt to nullify the air offensive that was bidding fair to strangle their submarine fleet, the enemy had resorted to the policy, ultimately disastrous to itself, of remaining surfaced during the attack and fighting back with antiaircraft fire. One B-24 was believed lost as a result of this action.

Much more serious was the opposition encountered from enemy aircraft, though just as indicative of the enemy's desperate plight. German aircraft over the Bay in July and August accounted for 2 aircraft and 14 lives. Ju-88s were encountered throughout the entire period of operations, often in very large groups. The average number was 6.6 enemy aircraft per encounter. It was therefore cause for surprise that so few planes of the 479th were lost. Even so, of course, the strain on the crews of the single B-24s in the face of such large groups was very great. Crews were instructed to avoid combat wherever possible, but in many instances the enemy pressed the attacks vigorously

It is not the province of this study to evaluate the entire Biscay offensive. It continued long after the AAF Antisubmarine Command had ceased to exist, and until the submarine menace itself had been substantially reduced.

But some assessment must be attempted, at least for the period during which AAF Antisubmarine squadrons participated. It has been suggested that the campaign was a failure. Certainly the tangible results obtained in August failed to measure up to those of July. In July, 26 per cent of all attacks made on U-boats were made in the Bay, and the B-24's of the Antisubmarine Command operating in that area had to fly an average of only 56 flying hours per sighting. The situation altered radically in August. Only seven damaging or destructive attacks were made in that month, as compared to 29 for July. Sightings fell off proportionately, and the 479th Antisubmarine Group certainly spent most of its time in August combating enemy aircraft rather than in attacking U-boats. Yet throughout the month of August, plotting boards regularly carried from 10 to 20 U-boats in the area, which is approximately the same concentration as characterized the previous month. Nor can the decrease be charged to any relaxation of the offensive effort.

The failure to sight the enemy in August may be explained in part as the result of the installation of radar by the Germans in their submarines. Increasingly, the aircraft on antisubmarine patrol found that the "blips" disappeared from their radar screens at average distances of 3 or 9 miles, indicating that the enemy was detecting patrol aircraft at safe distances. The Germans also altered their tactics considerably in order to cut down the heavy losses sustained by them in July. They abandoned the practice of remaining surfaced and fighting back during air attacks, and resorted again to an over-all policy of evasion, hugging the Spanish coastline so as to confuse radar contact, and surfacing only at night in that farthest-south part of the Bay which lat at the extreme limit of the English Wellingtons equipped with Leigh-lights. Some credit must also be given to the persistent use of aircraft to counter the pressure of the Allied air offensive.

Nevertheless, it must be remembered that the tactics to which the Germans reported — fighting back in July, hugging the Spanish coast in August, and using extremely heavy air cover in both months – are themselves eloquent evidence of the effectiveness of the Bay offensive. And the effect of antisubmarine activity cannot be determined entirely by the amount of damage directly inflicted on the enemy. The constant patrolling of the Bay forced the submarines to proceed so slowly through the transit area that their efficiency in the open sea was greatly reduced and the morale of their crews seriously impaired. Yet, even in terms of submarines sunk or damaged, the Bay campaign inflicted heavy loss on the enemy. During its most active 3 months (June to September) it accounted for the following score:

	By Aircraft	By surface craft or submarine
Sunk & probably sunk	19	4
Damaged	9	4

5

THE MOROCCAN SEA FRONTIER

Closely related to the Bay of Biscay offensive was the action in the Moroccan Sea Frontier. In fact, the two at times overlapped, aircraft from the latter reinforcing the campaign in the transit area, at least in its more southerly reaches. In any event, the antisubmarine warfare in the approaches to the Straits of Gibraltar was always likely to be affected by strategy in the Bay, probably even more than other Atlantic areas, all of which were affected in one way or another. As the summer Bay offensive reached its climax in late June and early July, the U-boats tended more and more to skirt the Spanish coast to Cape Finisterre, and from there to deploy in a southwesterly direction toward the waters between the Azores and the cost of Portugal. The result was a concentration, during the first 2 weeks of July, of enemy submarines in that area, which thus became part of the narrow transit lane.

It is a matter of question what exactly were the strategic motives back of this movement. Undoubtedly it sprang in large part simply from a desire to evade patrolling forces in the Bay. But it also appears to be true that the U-boats were spending considerable time in that region on anti-shipping patrol. It may very well have been that they were ordered to spend several days in these waters on their way to and from their Biscay bases. The object was apparently to create a person off the coast of Portugal to intercept

Allied convoys proceeding from the United Kingdom to supply the Allied campaign then being developed in the Mediterranean. It was a bold move, for it brought the U-boats within range of antisubmarine aircraft operating from Northwest Africa and Gibraltar, and it coincided with the brief and desperate attempt of the submarines in the Bay to counter the air offensive by antiaircraft fire. The enemy also relied on the relative ease with which air protection could be provided in the form of JU-88's and the longer range FW-200's. There is difference of opinion concerning the precise number of U-boats patrolling off the coast of Portugal in the first half of July, the estimate ranging from 8 to 25. But it is certain that a considerable concentration came within range of African-based Liberators.

It is at this point that the B-24's of the 480th Group reenter the picture. They had been moved to Port Lyautey in March and had extended the patrolled area in the Moroccan Sea Frontier by several hundred miles. There squadrons were specially equipped to answer the challenge made by the U-boats as the latter swung across the convoy lane in early July. Their offensive really began with a sighting on 5 July in which the pilot made a perfectly executed run on a submarine, but was foiled by mechanical failure of his bomb bay doors. On the 7th, two attacks were made, one of which resulted in the probable sinking of one U-boat. The other may also have been destroyed, although it was officially assessed as probably severely damaged. The following day a fifth attack occurred which resulted in another probable kill. On 9 July three attacks were delivered, one of which was assessed as severe damage, one as slight damage, and one as no damage at all. Next day another attack resulted in doubtful damage, and again on the 11th an attack of undetermined effect was executed. On the 12th, 13th, and 14th, an attack was made each day, resulting in one submarine definitely destroyed and two damaged. Thus, during this short period of 10 days, the 2 squadrons made 15 sighting s and 13 attacks, which are believed to have resulted in 1 submarine known sunk, 3 probably sunk, 2 severely damaged, and 1 possibly damaged. Only 6 attacks were considered unsuccessful.

After this decisive, if local, defeat, the enemy obviously decided to abandon his policy of active defense. The U-boats now dived, whenever possible, on sight of antisubmarine aircraft, and not a single submarine was sighted by AAF aircraft in the area thereafter. It was also immediately after this brief "blitz" that the Germans began to patrol the area with heavily armed FW-200's, and it is logical to presume that the action of the 480th Group had a good deal to do with that development.

In order to put this July offensive in its proper perspective, it will be necessary to review the history of operations in the Moroccan Sea Frontier from the time when Col. Jack Roberts and his 480th Antisubmarine Group reported at Port Lyautey in March 1943.

The 480th Group encountered in Africa something more than the usual problems involved in transfer to a new theater. Most of the difficulties arose from the fact that the group was now placed under the operational control of the US Navy. It was assigned to the Northwest African Coastal Air Force for administration, and attacked temporarily to Fleet Air Wing 13 for operational control, pending decision as to the control and disposition of all Allied antisubmarine units in Northwest Africa and Gibraltar. Colonel Roberts felt that this arrangement was most unsatisfactory for several reasons. The group had been the first of the AAF Antisubmarine Command units to operate free from US naval control. It had been thoroughly indoctrinated in RAF Coastal Command procedures, which differed markedly from those of the US Navy, and the officers of the group felt that, for the job at hand, they were much superior. Morale was adversely affected by poorer radio communications, less efficient briefing, and operational control, poorer air-sea rescue facilities than those to which the unit had become accustomed. An example of the resulting friction was that, with five intelligence officers capable and experienced in briefing and interrogating crews, the group was not allowed to provide watch in the control room or to conduct briefing. Since the briefing provided by Fleet Air Wing 15 was not considered adequate by Colonel Roberts, crews had to be re-briefed by an officer of the group before going on a mission. Worse than that, intelligence data necessary for successful missions frequently got to the group too late to be of any real value. And, with practically no operational authority, there was little that Colonel Roberts could do about it. Nor was much attention being paid to estimated u-boat positions in routing patrol aircraft, which resulted in poorly planned missions. In general, it was felt that the best use was not being made of a highly trained organization.

Basically, the trouble lay in the difference of strategic thinking between Navy and AAF Antisubmarine Command:

The unsatisfactory nature of our present status and operations is due (Colonel Roberts wrote in May) … to the difference in the Fundamental conception of Moroccan Sea Frontier and this Hqtrs as to how best to defeat the submarines, whether offensively (on sweeps and covering threatened convoys) or defensively (covering all US convoys at all times to the exclusion of offensive sweeps and coverage's).

As will appear in the following pages, the Navy had performed its initial function adequately by patrolling the approaches to Gibraltar to within 400 miles and had helped to force the Germans beyond that limit. But the long-range and very-long-range aircraft of the Antisubmarine Command had a new and different mission to perform, namely, that of reaching beyond the 400-mile line and striking the submarines prowling in the outer waters. The two missions thus required two different approaches, a fact which the Moroccan Sea Frontier failed to appreciate.

Since the problem of command in the Gibraltar-Northwest African area was currently under discussion in the spring of 1943, Colonel Roberts vigorously urged, as a solution, placing antisubmarine operations in the area under British control at Gibraltar. The RAF Coastal Command was operating antisubmarine squadrons from both Gibraltar and Agadir – to the north and south of Port Lyautey respectively. So he believed the best interests of all concerned would be served by coordinating operations from all three bases under Coastal Command control. "I am … convinced," he wrote in May, "as are all of my subordinates, that our Wing can operate 'independently' under the central control of AOS Gibraltar with much greater efficiency and effectiveness than under present US Navy control." This statement, he warned, was made without malice toward any individuals of the Navy "hereabouts," for were "generally a fine bunch with whom our relations are on a most pleasant basis." He then added, significantly, "The majority of them privately concur with me in my expressed ideas on antisubmarine organization in Northwest Africa."

The breakthrough. The B-24 Liberator bomber was modified for antisubmarine patrol and U-boat attack. As a long range heavy bomber the B-24 brought a lethal load or depth charges, torpedoes and machine gun fire to bear on the Nazi submarines. Credit: United States Air Force.

A two ship of B-24s patrol north of Amsterdam towards the convoy routes to Russia.

The aptly names Biscay Belle patrolled the Bay of Biscay. Note the light colored paint applied to the bottom of the bomber. This helped it blend in with the sky.

An aerial photograph of the German sub base at La Rochelle, France. The U-boat pens are inside the breakwater.

Half the battle was to cut off the arrival of new U-boats at the source and
that required raids against the German shipyards by the heavy bombers
of the Eighth Air Force. This previously unpublished photograph is of the
shipyards at Hamburg. In it you can see seven U-boats under construction,
all damaged by a recent air attack. (Mighty Eighth Air Force Museum)

Four U-boat hulls can be clearly seen at the top right in this previously
unpublished photograph of the German shipyards at Bremen (Mighty Eighth
Air Force Museum)

Convoy in the Atlantic.
Official US Coast Guard Photograph

An allied tanker splits in two after being torpedoed in the Atlantic. 1942.
National Archives

The well-known painting of an attack created by LCDR Anton Otto Fischer. National Archives.

This page and next. A Canadian warship hunts down a German submarine forced to surface and now attempting to flee. Canadian War Museum

The USS Spencer captures the U-175.
Courtesy: The United States Coast Guard

On 17 April 1943, the U.S.S. Spencer, C.G., escorting Convoy HX-233 to the United Kingdom, located the submerged U-175 as the cutter steamed ahead of the convoy. Attacking quickly, the cutter's depth charges severely damaged the U-boat, forcing the Germans to surface. The Spencer, her sister cutter Duane, and many of the merchant ships in the convoy, then opened fire on the U-175 as soon as the submarine broke the ocean's surface. The U-boat's crew attempted to abandon the submarine despite the heavy fire. The U-boat's commanding officer was killed in the initial hail of gunfire but ultimately 41 Germans were rescued safely. There were two combat photographers aboard the cutters, Jack January aboard Spencer and Bob Gates aboard Duane, and they captured the action on film, giving posterity a close-up view of the death of one of Hitler's U-boats during the height of the Battle of the Atlantic.

The following four pages: Official US Coast Guard Photographs

Below. The USS Spencer as seen from the cutter Duane.

Depth charges wound the German submarine. Note the convoy in the distance.

The sub surfaces and is caught in a hail of bullets and shells.

The German sailors abandon ship. The submarine's captain has been killed in action but 41 survivors are rescued.

Two German submarines are swept ashore in the aftermath of a heavy thunderstorm. Falmouth, England. Sometime after the end of World War II. National Archives

A captured German U-boat crew.

A German U-boat crewman waits to be fished from the ocean.

This U-boat has been captured and taken into tow. Note the US flag.

In fact, by June, improvement was becoming evident in the general control exercised by Fleet Air Wing 15, and in the quality of services furnished at Port Lyautey, although no change in the official status of the group, or in the quantity of services, had taken place. Group intelligence officers were being given equal authority and responsibility with naval, and air-ground liaison was "reasonably satisfactory." Army and Navy intelligence officers were rotating duty shifts in the Control Room. And the group was exercising increased authority, "actually if not officially," in the laying out of patrols, "the Navy exhibiting little interest in anything other than convoy coverage."

The Navy did not, of course, furnish all the problems facing the 480th Group in Africa, though it provided the largest of them. In addition to the myriad of problems incident on stationing several hundred men in a strange territory and climate, Colonel Roberts had to build up his unit from a strength of not more than 16 or 17 VLR aircraft to one of 24 VLR (E). This increase in aircraft, especially in the modified B-24D, involved considerable training of crews both old and new, and considerable adjustment of equipment. As of 23 June 1943, the group reported 19 VLR (E) aircraft on hand, with 6 en route from the United States.

The 480th Group arrived in Africa as a well-trained unit. Thanks to the experience gained under the tutelage of the Coastal Command, the group officers felt that their organization was better prepared for antisubmarine tasks than any other American unit. And the quality of the new crews received from the OUT at Langley Field had steadily improved. The chief training problem consequently arose in connection with the new equipment being received and the unfamiliar flying conditions prevailing in the Moroccan Sea Frontier, where scarcity of clouds made tactics learned under the heavier northern skies inapplicable. The commanding officer was especially conscious of the value of continuous training, and, once such facilities as a triangulation bombing range and a blind-landing system had been set up, he maintained a steady training schedule.

Morale constituted an ever-present, though happily not a serious, problem. At first the crews felt insecure under that they considered inferior radio control from the Navy, and in view of the fact that rescue facilities were lacking. Recreation facilities remained limited, relaxation consisting mainly of athletics and an earnest endeavor to consume enough liquor before 2330 to make a pas, normally expiring at that hour, worth the trouble of securing. Unfortunately, the 480th Group was the only "front line" unit in what was considered to be a rear echelon, or rest area, and the Provost Marshal persisted in subjecting it to the same type of restrictions ordinarily imposed on inactive units. Morale in general, however, remained high until, in August, rumors of the impending dissolution of the AAF Antisubmarine Command left all personnel in an uncertain and frustrated frame of mind.

The 480th Antisubmarine Group found in the Moroccan Sea Frontier a field especially well suited to its talents. Since the invasion of Africa on 5 November 1942, a major objective of the German submarine fleet had been to harry Allied convoys heading for the Northwest Africa and Gibraltar. At first they had met with some success. On 11 November 1942, four merchant vessels and one destroyer were sunk while riding at anchor off Pedala (20 miles from Casablanca) by what appears to have been a mass U-boat attack. Allied aircraft, however, soon made hunting in threes shore-line waters too costly for the enemy to continue. This work had largely been done by the British who made 37 sightings between 7 and 30 November, resulting in 21 attacks. By the end of December the PEY's had made 7 attacks in the area. The result was that the enemy retired to positions 400 miles or more from Casablanca and Port Lyautey. Instead of having to guard only a 200-mile span, the U-boats then had to guard an arc several hundred miles long; and for some time they actually took up positions along the arc of an approximate circle centered at Gibraltar. After January, all sinking's occurred more than 600 miles from the nearest aircraft base. During all this time the U-boats showed little tendency to approach within range of land-based aircraft, for, although thousands of hours were flown, no sightings were made until the arrival of the Liberators in March. These long-range aircraft were able to reach both the U-boats on patrol beyond PBY range and also those traveling the great-circle submarine lanes to South America and South Africa. During the period March to June, a total of 12 sightings were made, mostly beyond the 400-mile limit. Meanwhile, aircraft operations from Casablanca had been discontinued and PBY's began patrols from Agadir in April. By June, the location of American antisubmarine forces in the Moroccan Sea Frontier was approximately as follows:

Port Lyautey	Army	15	(480th Antisubmarine Group)
	Navy	12	(VP-92 and part of VP-73)
Agadir	Navy	6	(remainder of VP-73)

Thus it became the peculiar task of the 480th Group to carry on long-distance patrols, beyond the extreme range of the PBY's, making the maximum use of the SCR-517 radar. Missions began promptly on 19 March in spite of temporary shortages of spare parts, maintenance personnel, and equipment. Three planes a day ordinarily went out on operational missions, laid out by Fleet Air Wing 15, under the supervision of the Moroccan Sea Frontier at Casablanca. The area covered was at first from 31 degrees N. to 35 degrees W., extending west to the prudent limit of endurance (1050 nautical miles). Later missions were ordered almost as far north as Cape Finisterre. Within 2 days of the beginning operations, the group made the first sighting that had occurred in the area since December, and in the ensuing months of its stay at Port Lyautey it made roughly 10 times as many sightings per hour of flying time as the Navy PBY's operating from the same region at the same time. This result was owing in part to the extra range of the B-24, but also to the alert visual search of the B-24 crews and to the superior efficiency of their radar, which came nearer than the PBY equipment to making the theoretically expected number of sightings in the patrolled regions by a factor of 4.

Of these sightings, all made in the period March to July 1943, inclusive, more than 90 per cent resulted in attacks on U-boats, and of these 20 attacks, 10 per cent were sure kills. In all, more than 25 per cent of the U-boats attacked probably failed to reach port. Assessments run as follows:

2 U-boats known sunk

3 U-boats probably sunk

1 U-boat probably or severely damaged

5 U-boats possibly or slightly damaged

9 U-boats no damage or insufficient evidence of damage

This fine record in largely owing to the high quality of flying technique and sound tactics employed by the pilots, to the well-coordinated use of radar, and to the aggressiveness of the crews. Especially noteworthy is the use made of cloud cover. Clouds were available for use in 73 per cent of the sightings, and were actually used in nearly 60 per cent. In other words, of the 16 sightings in which cloud cover was available, it was used in 13 cases. Of the other 3, 2 involved flying below clouds on convoy coverage, and the other flying below clouds in darkness, both perfectly correct procedure.

As a result of superior flying technique, 16 of the 20 attacks were made while the enemy craft was still visible, and in 13 instances the U-boat was still fully surfaced or with decks awash at the time of attack. Here the B-24's again surpassed the PBY's for , in all but 2 of the 13 sightings made by the latter from November to 15 July, the U-boats were able to submerge before the arrival of the aircraft. In one of these instances, the submarine deliberately chose to remain surfaced and fight back with AA fire. This result arose in part from the slower speed of the Navy planes and from less effective radar.

At least 12 of the sightings made by the group were first picked up by the SGB-517 radar equipment at an average range of 18 miles. At least 5 of these sightings would certainly not have been made without radar, and in 6 others the contact would otherwise have been doubtful.

The spirit of the crews played a very large part in securing the high record of attacks and kills. They showed general willingness to encounter enemy fire and an ability to carry out attacks in the face of strong opposition. In six instances the submarines fired on the attacking planes, yet with the exception of the first case in which resistance occurred, the aircraft pressed home their attacks. Several planes were damaged by this sort of encounter, and about 12 crew members injured.

As in the Bay of Biscay, encounters with enemy aircraft in the Moroccan Sea Frontier proved more serious than resistance from the submarines themselves. As in the Bay, also, the early operations of the group were not seriously opposed by enemy aircraft, but opposition became more and more severe as the effectiveness of the antisubmarine patrols increased. In the Moroccan Sea Frontier it was not the relatively short-range JU-68 that opposed the aircraft of the 480th Group but the powerful long-range PW-200, which in many ways is comparable to the B-24 itself. The first combats of this nature occurred in the last half of July, when the antisubmarine "blitz" conducted by the 480th Group during the first 2 weeks had goaded the enemy into desperate action. By August the FW-200's began to appear, heavily armed with rapid-firing 20-millimeter cannon which gave them a marked fire superiority over the B-24. From that point on, the crews of the 420th found their mission to be very hazardous, and the casualties increased rapidly. The final record is, however, one of which the group may well be proud, for, during its entire African operations, through October 1943, it is estimated to have destroyed 5 FW-200's, 2 DC-34's, and 1 DC-26; probably destroyed 1 Ju-88; and damaged 2 FW-200's and 2 JU-88's. In doing so the group lost 3 B-24's as a result of action by enemy aircraft.

In all, the 480th Group put in a more than satisfactory amount of work in the Moroccan Sea Frontier prior to the dissolution of the Antisubmarine Command, even allowing for the excellent flying weather prevailing in the area. The following table demonstrates this feat:

	Anti-submarine Sweep	Convoy coverage	Total hours flown
March	400	–	400
April	1123	397	1519
May	674	733	1407
June	1119	541	1660
July	1544	624	2163
August	883	795	1678

This table also demonstrates the relatively high proportion of flying time devoted to escorting convoys, a type of operation unlikely to produce many sightings of enemy submarines. From November 1942 to the middle of July 1943, no unthreatened convoy (defined as one having no plotted U-boat positions within 100 miles, or within 100 miles of its course for the ensuing 24 hours) was attacked. Conversely, of the 22 sightings made by aircraft in the area between 5 December and 15 July 1943 over 90 per cent occurred within 30 miles of a plotted U-boat position. The average error was only 41 miles.

Facts of this sort confirmed the officers of the 480th Group in their belief that their aircraft would be much more profitably employed in hunting in areas of high probability (defined as regions enclosed by arcs of circles, 50 miles in radius, drawn about predicted U-boat positions) than in convoy coverage. They recognized, of course, that their very long range allowed them to pick up convoys much farther out to sea than was otherwise possible, a practice which the convoy commanders greatly favored. And it was also true that a minimum of actual danger from unpiloted submarines made a certain minimum of air coverage advisable on all convoys. Nevertheless, the results obtained in areas of high probability more than justified the diversion of as many planes as possible in those directions. Since such areas occurred mainly out of range of the naval planes (beyond the 500-mile limit) they fell principally to the Army B-24's. As experience was gained, it became evident that by far the best ratio of hours per sighting could be obtained beyond 500 miles and on adroitly routed missions. As the Army became more and more influential, officially or unofficially, in routing patrols, a gradual improvement in that respect took place.

The campaign of 5-15 July, narrated above, gave the group a splendid opportunity to prove not only its fighting ability but the validity of these tactical principles. Deployed on missions carefully routed toward those areas off the Portuguese coast where intelligence sources indicated the enemy had concentrated its forces, the aircraft of the group turned in what is probably a record for a unit of the sort.

The effect of this campaign of July may be estimated to some extent by the fact that, after 14 July, the 480th Group made no further contacts with enemy submarines during their stay on the west coast of Africa. The Germans' attempt to defy heavy air coverage had proved disastrous to themselves and it was once again demonstrated that submarines either could not or would not operate in areas at all well covered by antisubmarine aircraft. In August patrols and convoy protective flights continued and were even extended. Employing tactics similar to those used by the RAF Coastal Command in July, a "shuttle run" was made in the early part of the month by the 2d Squadron between Fort Lyautey and Dunkeswell. On the trip to Dunkeswell the squadron covered a convoy; and on the return flight it conducted an antisubmarine sweep, thus combining two principal functions in one operation. Two such runs were made in August, but no submarines were attacked.

The antisubmarine warfare in the Moroccan Sea Frontier generally may be similarly evaluated. Between the British squadrons at Gibraltar and the navy squadrons in the Moroccan Sea Frontier, the Allied antisubmarine forces had, prior to the arrival of the Army B-24's, forced the enemy to withdraw from the immediate approaches to the vital area. The operations of the 480th Group forced them to withdraw to a point at which they could no longer seriously menace the convoys pouring through the Moroccan Sea Frontier, bound for the Mediterranean theater. And in July, when convoys were sailing down from the United Kingdom to supply the Sicilian campaign, they were able to pass through the greatest concentration of U-boats then at sea without loss from submarine activity, thanks to the effective air and surface escort provided. This relative immunity granted finally to the Moroccan and Gibraltar area was a triumph for combined convoy escort and offensive antisubmarine sweeps, and it vindicated the principles underlying each form of antisubmarine activity within its own peculiar limits.

The operations in the Eastern Atlantic were experimental in a great many ways. For one thing, they gave the AAF Antisubmarine Command the opportunity to test its strategic doctrine. In the course of their rather brief duration, experiments were carried out in the difficult matter of administering the activities of units operating far from their parent organizations, and in the even more difficult problem of operational control. And, by no means least of all, invaluable experience was obtained in antisubmarine tactics in an area where operations had to be conducted on a more than theoretical scale.

As a result of these efforts, the AAF Antisubmarine Command was able to draw certain interesting, if tentative, conclusions. The offensive strategy had worked. If not the be-all and end-all of antisubmarine warfare, it had at least to be considered an essential element. In administration, the policy of sending units on detached service from the wing headquarters in the United States soon proved to be unsound and was replaced by one in which the overseas squadrons were given "separate, special" group organization. An effort had been made to extend that principle to the point of creating overseas wings, but AAF headquarters was opposed to expanding the AAF Antisubmarine Command organization on such a scale. Operational control had been exercised over the AAF Antisubmarine Command units by both RAF Coastal Command and US Navy. The comparison was striking, and not always to the advantage of the latter. The AAF Antisubmarine Command had always recognized its British counterpart as a pattern, and the experience of actual cooperation under the operational control of the older organization had only confirmed the younger in its preference. Yet even in Northwest Africa the problem of naval control was greatly mitigated, if not exactly solved, as a result of the tact and vigor of the commanders involved. Finally, the detached antisubmarine units learned more in a week of operations in the eastern Atlantic about such things as defense against aircraft attack, proper attack procedures, and the use of cloud cover and radar equipment than they could have done in weeks of operations elsewhere. It was with a sense of anticlimax and frustration that they heard, in August 1943, that they were to be relieved of their mission just when they felt they were really achieving their objective and when they were, in fact, as efficient an antisubmarine team as could be found at that time.

6

OPERATIONS IN THE WESTERN ATLANTIC

The Eastern and Gulf Sea Frontiers. In contrast to the intensive, if sporadic, activity of the overseas squadrons, the story of antisubmarine operations in the western Atlantic is one of endless patrols, few sightings, and still fewer attacks. While the units of the 479th and 480th Antisubmarine Groups were enjoying the best of hunting in the Bay of Biscay and in the Moroccan Sea Frontier, flying at worst only a few hundred hours per contact, units in many parts of the US strategic area were flying many thousands of hours per sighting in regions with an average U-boat density of 1 in a million square miles of ocean. In the Eastern and Gulf Sea Frontiers almost no enemy activity had been encountered since September 1942. To the south and north, in the Trinidad area, and in that part of the North Atlantic convoy route lying off the coast of Newfoundland, the Germans were still trying hard to stop the flow of vital material. Even in these areas, however, the hunting was often poor.

Yet the Navy felt obliged to patrol not only these threatened areas but the relatively quiet waters of the Eastern and Gulf Sea Frontiers with as many aircraft as might be spared from other more urgent projects. The enemy, it was argued, had withdrawn, but he might return. He was not too preoccupied with the invasion convoys to overlook a rich and unprotected merchant shipping lane. And, as Admiral King put it, the submarines could shift their area of operation more rapidly than the air defenses could be moved to meet them. Accordingly, an "irreducible minimum" of aircraft would have to be maintained on the coast of the United States, despite the meager returns in contacts with the enemy.

The only question was, how small did that minimum have to be before it became truly irreducible? Was it necessary to provide such heavy coverage – at one time as many as 15 out of 25 squadrons? Was it an economical way of using units specially trained in the work of destroying submarines to deploy them in areas where there were few if any submarines, when in other parts of the Atlantic the undersea raiders abounded? These were debatable questions, the debate resolving itself finally into a conflict between the AAF Antisubmarine Command ideal of a mobile offensive force and the Navy's doctrine of a relatively fixed defense. Since the operational control of antisubmarine activity lay in naval hands, the Navy won the debate. The result was that many of the fully trained and equipped antisubmarine crews could say of their operations as one squadron historian said, somewhat wistfully, of his entire squadron: "The tactical achievement of the squadron cannot be elaborated on by enumerating the number of submarines sunk. It has been our misfortune never to have had the opportunity of sighting a submarine." When he added sturdily that "this fact has never reduced the crews' efficiency and patrol missions have been conducted in an alert manner," he epitomized a large portion of this story.

This work of patrol and convoy escort was shared by AAF Antisubmarine Command, air units of the US Navy, and the Civilian Air Patrol. It must be remembered, however, that the CAP planes were light, single-engine civilian types, limited in their range to a narrow zone along the coast where the depth of the water normally restricted submarine activity, and that the planes used by the Navy in the Eastern Sea Frontier were mostly single-motor observation types, with a limited radius of action compared to the Navy PBY and the medium and heavy bombers used by the Antisubmarine Command.

From October 1942 to February 1943, no damaging attacks were made in the Eastern and Gulf Sea Frontiers, and few positive sightings of enemy submarines. This startling lack of combat action was by no means the result of any reduction in antisubmarine patrol activity which remained heavy on the part of both Army and navy squadrons. It was simply that there were few, if any, U-boats to see. From an estimated 10 enemy craft in August 1943, the average density in these areas had dropped in October to 3.4 and was further lowered in November to 1.7. In December, January, and February there was no positive evidence of any enemy activity at all, though some depth bombs were dropped on suspicious spots in the water. In all, these operations during the winter of 1942-43 probably did more damage to the aboriginal marine life in the patrolled areas than to the mechanized intruders. But there is no doubt that the negligible density of enemy submarines in its turn resulted partly from the continued heavy air coverage.

The spring and summer months of 1943 brought some increase in enemy operations. In February, the average density rose to 1.8, a significant increase if still not a major threat in over a million square miles of ocean. For the rest of the time the AAF Antisubmarine Command patrolled these frontiers, the Germans kept from one to three U-boats busy – and not without effect. In addition to keeping a disproportionately large antisubmarine force patrolling these waters, they managed in May to destroy the first merchant vessel sunk in the Eastern Sea Frontier since July 1942. Naval aircraft and a B-25 were in the vicinity of the attack on the tanker Pan Am (a straggler from another convoy) but were unable to make contact with the submarine. A U-boat, possibly the one that sank the Pan Am, was detected several times and was attacked by a Navy plane with possible damage resulting to it. Later in the month, a B-24 from the 18th Antisubmarine Squadron based at Langley Field, VA, made a fairly promising attack in the same general area. Again in June the tanker Gettysburg was sunk by a submarine (31 degrees 00' N. 79 degrees 00'W.). A Navy blimp had been escorting the tanker until separated from it by a thunderstorm. A plane of the 25th Antisubmarine Squadron later directed a passenger ship to the 15 survivors. In July the Bloody Marsh, a US tanker, met a similar fate. In August a patrol vessel was sunk (37 degrees 22'N. 74 degrees 25' W.). On the 28th of August a B-25 of the 25th Antisubmarine Squadron attacked a U-boat (31 degrees 31' N. 78 degrees 45' W.). Unfortunately, the enemy managed to escape before any serious damage could be dealt it.

In spite of the poor hunting in the Eastern and Gulf Sea Frontiers, the range and efficiency of the AAF Antisubmarine Command Squadrons in the area were gradually being increased by the substitution of B-24's for the medium-range aircraft originally employed, and by constant processing of crews, old as well as new, in the Operational Training Unit at Langley Field. By March 1943, the effect of increased long-range aircraft was becoming evident in an increase of over 3000 flying hours in the month for Army planes. On the 23d of that month, 23 B-24's were reported, distributed among the 4th, 6th, 9th, and 18th Squadrons. By August it was possible to report 75 B-24's among 9 of the squadrons based in the United States.

If this were the whole story of operations in the Eastern and Gulf Sea Frontiers – and as far as actual contact with the enemy is concerned, it is the whole story – it would be a disproportionately small one in relation to the number of squadrons involved. And it might seem strange that so great an effort was being made to increase precious long-range equipment in what was essentially an inactive theater. Happily the story is much larger, for it includes also a prodigious program of technical development and crew training. When the Antisubmarine Command war activated, a beginning only had been made in the task of occurring the proper weapons and auxil- iary devices for antisubmarine warfare, and of training personnel in their use. Close liaison had to be maintained between the command and the var- ious research organizations, and the new command had to put into effect a training program that was at once uniform and flexible enough to keep up with the constantly developing methods of antisubmarine warfare.

The responsibility in both material development and training rested not only on headquarters but also on the squadrons based in the continental United States, for it was with their help alone that the dual program could be implemented. It was originally contemplated that the Operational Training Unit at Langley Field would accomplish most of the training work for the entire command; but that objective was never completely achieved because the tremendous need for available aircraft made it necessary to carry on training to a considerable extent in conjunction with patrol opera- tions. Even when the flow of personnel through the OUT had become fuller and steadier, stress was still placed on squadron training. The US coastal area constituted a more or less inactive theater and it was felt that those squadrons tied down to patrol over those waters could profitable be used to supplement the training program. Training, therefore, became the principal contribution made by the home-based units. The story of this program will be told in a later chapter.

7

THE CARIBBEAN AND SOUTH ATLANTIC AREAS

As the Command withdrew their submarines from the Eastern and Gulf Sea Frontiers, during the late summer of 1942, they concentrated for a time in the Caribbean area, specializing in the waters off Trinidad. The Caribbean had been a favorite hunting ground for the enemy since his entry in force into the US strategic area. By September 1942, however, the convoy lanes off Trinidad offered one of the few profitable areas of operations in the western Atlantic. During the winter months, the Caribbean shared with the northern coastal waters a relative immunity from submarine attack. In December and January, a total of 10 merchant vessels were sunk, all outside the Caribbean, in the area east of Trinidad. In February, none were lost. In March, five sinking's occurred in the Caribbean, the first in the island ring since September. During the following months, from one to four enemy submarines were kept in the area, seldom, however, doing much damage.

The enemy withdrawal from the Caribbean, late in 1943, was part of the same strategic movement that took the submarines from the Eastern and Gulf Sea Frontiers. Unable to continue his original policy of destroying Allied shipping faster than it could be replaced, Admiral Doenitz had withdrawn the bulk of his submarine fleet in an attempt to fend off the "invasion" convoy. But it was apparently also a part of his strategic plan to leave a minimum force of U-boats in convoy and shipping areas of secondary importance. The nuisance value of these scattered raiders was enormous, for they kept a large force of surface craft and aircraft tied down to convoy coverage and routine patrol. In accomplishing this effect, only an occasional merchant vessel had to be sunk, and the operation could be carried on with the least possible risk to the submarine, since it could proceed in a leisurely fashion, evading searching patrols wherever possible.

The problem, then, was to provide enough effective air coverage for the Caribbean to keep the U-boat threat to a minimum. For, no matter how greatly motives of high strategy had figured in the withdrawal of the enemy from the American areas, the fact still remained that the Germans normally stayed out of reach of effective air patrol, and deliberately sought out those areas in which it was lacking. So, from the beginning of its career, the AAF Antisubmarine Command was requested to plan for the deployment of an effective force in the Caribbean areas.

Operations in the Cuban area were undertaken in accordance with an agreement between the US and Cuban governments drawn up 19 June 1943, and were controlled directly from Headquarters, 26th Antisubmarine Wing, Miami, FL. These operations, undertaken successively by the 23d, the 8th, the 17th, and the 15th Antisubmarine Squadrons, supplemented those of the squadrons based in the Florida and Gulf areas. The net result was similar to that obtained by the squadrons based in the United States. Yet, as in other coastal waters, the enemy continued to keep a few U-boats operating in the Cuban area and managed to sink a few ships. In July 1943 a probable strength of four U-boats accounted for two merchant vessels. It was felt, therefore, that an antisubmarine squadron of the AAF Antisubmarine Command should be kept in that region.

A similar, though somewhat more exciting story, may be told of operations in the Trinidad area through which passed probably three-fourths of the Caribbean shipping. Pioneer work in this part of the world had been done for the AAF Antisubmarine Command squadrons by the 40th Bombardment Squadron, later designated the 4th Antisubmarine Squadron. From August to November 1943, that unit had threaded its way among the intricacies of command channels in the Caribbean Sea Frontier and had at least prepared succeeding squadrons for the sort of problem they were likely to face.

And problems in plenty they faced, too. The weather itself proved a serious handicap to sustained operations, what with tropical hurricanes and torrential rain falls; and night maintenance had to be entirely abandoned because of the prevalence of malaria-bearing mosquitoes. If a pilot were unfortunate enough to be forced into a jungle landing, he might never get out alive. One pilot landed in the jungle at Zanderij Field, Dutch Guiana, only 15 minutes from his base. After 4 days of hard work a rescue party reached him. On top of all this, the native population of Trinidad either disliked the Americans or British with an intensity that promised little in the way of hospitality, or else their unusually high venereal disease rate promised a little too much.

The most serious problem came, however, not from the climate or the native population, but from the command situation into which the AAF Antisubmarine Command squadrons were plunged. Being on detached service from the 25th Wing, these squadrons had to be given a place in the administrative and operational structure already set up in the region; but, being temporary in statue and late in arriving, they found no very satisfactory place in that system. As in the Eastern and Gulf Sea Frontiers, antisubmarine activity was under the operational control of the sea Frontier commander. AAF Antisubmarine Command squadrons were placed under the administrative supervision of the area defense command. But in addition to the Caribbean Sea Frontier and the Caribbean Defense Command, many lesser headquarters existed between the highest echelon and the single AAF Antisubmarine Command squadron serving at Trinidad. Under the Caribbean Defense Command, air forces were normally administered by the Sixth Air Force, but, since the latter had delegated all its antisubmarine functions to the Antilles Air Task Force, all Army aircraft engaged in that work were under the jurisdiction of the Task Force. The 25th Bomb Group, with its headquarters at Trinidad, was attached to the Trinidad Detachment of the Antilles Air Task Force, and it was to this group that the AAF Antisubmarine Command squadrons were assigned. This, more or less, was the chain of command for administration. Air force supply and higher echelon maintenance came from the Trinidad Area Air Service Command under the Trinidad Sector Command.

On the operational aide, the jurisdiction of the Caribbean Sea Frontier, to which the Antilles Air Task Force had been assigned, was almost entirely decentralized among four sub regions at Guantanamo, Puerto Rico, Trinidad, and Curacao. Between these subordinate commands, communications appear to have been somewhat cumbersome, and coordination frequently slow or entirely lacking. Such an operational structure would have been perfectly adequate as a system of static defense, but in antisubmarine operations, which demanded the highest possible mobility based on the most rapid and complete transmission of intelligence possible, it proved to be much less suitable, and no doubt led to a less economical use of the antisubmarine forces available than might otherwise have been the case. Even more annoying to headquarters was its inability to order units into the Caribbean, or to exchange units, without securing specific authority from the Joint Command in Washington, and without having given advance notice of the movement to the Commander, Caribbean Sea Frontier and having secured concurrence from him or any other interested Caribbean headquarters. With submarines likely to make their appearance suddenly and in force, this was an awkward arrangement since it bound the officer commanding AAF Antisubmarine Command units in the area to the point where he could not act quickly enough to counter such a move.

Operations from Edinburgh Field, Trinidad, were controlled more or less directly from Naval Operating Base, Trinidad, located at Fort of Spain, the air officer of which had final decision concerning the time and nature of each mission. Control over operations was exercised from a joint control room, established on lines similar to those at Miami and New York City. Information was received by headquarters, 25th Bomb Group, at Edinburgh Field, and from a local control room relayed to the AAF Antisubmarine Command squadron stationed there.

The first antisubmarine command squadron to go to Trinidad was the 9th. The air echelon, consisting of 42 officers and 73 enlisted men in 10 B-16R type planes, arrived at Edinburgh Field on 2 December 1942, Maj. Glendon P. Overing in command. Living conditions at the field were generally considered good, possibly better than in Miami. In addition to the 9th

Antisubmarine Squadron, the 10th Bombardment Squadron, a flight of the 417th Bombardment Squadron, and some Navy blimps operated from the field, all on primarily antisubmarine duty. Patrol missions began at once for the B-13's. To the chagrin of all present, the number of submarines active in the Trinidad area declined sharply after the arrival of the 9th Squadron. In January 1943 no vessels were sunk in the waters around Trinidad, as compared to 5 in December and 13 in November. And it is very doubtful whether the increased air coverage provided by the 9th did more than confirm the Germans in a policy of strategic withdrawal already agreed upon, or possible hasten the rate of that retreat. As the threat of a U-boat concentration decreased, sweeps gave way to convoy coverage, and some tactical time was given up to an accelerated training program.

Equipped with aircraft of medium range only, and patrolling an area in which seldom more than one U-boat operated, the 9th Squadron could hardly be expected to turn in a long list of attacks. Prior to its return to the United States in the latter part of March 1943, it had, however, made seven sightings and two attacks, both probably embarrassing to the enemy. In fact, in March, though flying only one-tenth of the total hours flown in the Trinidad area, it was fortunate enough to record three of the four sightings made during the month in those waters.

The 9th Squadron had been separated from its ground echelon for 3 months. During that time it had gained a great deal of experience in use of radar and in operational flying. It was decided that the squadron should be reunited and given transition training in long-range aircraft in order to make the best use of this experience. The air echelon of the 7th Antisubmarine Squadron and part of the ground echelon were accordingly ordered to Trinidad to replace the 9th.

With 10 radar-equipped B-18's, the 7th continued the work of patrolling the convoy lance, both those from the west and those, especially of the bauxite ships, plying along the South American coast. Occasionally, convoys passed to the north and northeast of the island and, in order to provide more complete coverage, planes would be sent to St. Lucia and to Barbados for several days. Although from 4 to 12 patrols were flown daily, weather permitting, and three-fourths of the time with radar equipment, the 7th Squadron had even less luck than the 9th in making contact with the enemy.

From the end of March until the middle of July, when it was relieved by the 8th, the 7th Squadron obtained only one contact and made no attacks. In fact, the only unusual incident resulted when the delicate political situation in Martinique required that the squadron patrol the island, two planes having been based at St. Lucia for that purpose.

In July 1943 the enemy staged what amounted to a concerted offensive in the Trinidad area. The average density of U-boats increased to 4 daily, sinking's of merchant vessels increased to 4, and attacks on submarines reached 13. Of these attacks, the 8th Antisubmarine Squadron, having stationed flights of B-24's at Zandorij and Waller Fields to cope with the situation, accounted for 3. Of the rest, 4 were made by – 18's of the 35th Bombardment Squadron stationed at Zanderij, and 7 by Navy planes. It is interesting to note that this flurry of activity coincided with the desperate efforts of the Germans in the eastern Atlantic to proceed in spite of air coverage. In 10 of the July attacks the enemy elected to fight back.

None of the three attacks delivered by the B-24D aircraft of the 8th Antisubmarine Squadron resulted in direct damage to the submarine, but twice they participated in effective killer-hunts.

On 31 August, the 8th Squadron was replaced by the 23d, which undertook experimental operations in the area with 16 D-35G aircraft equipped with the debatable 75-millimeter cannon in the nose. The withdrawal of the AAF Antisubmarine Command from antisubmarine patrol, in August 1943, left these operations still inconclusive.

The Caribbean and the South Atlantic areas both seemed to AAF Antisubmarine Command planners a fertile field for expansion. Early plane had included these areas. An effort was also made in 1943 to establish a separate antisubmarine wing in the Caribbean in order to provide administrative machinery for a large-scale operation in that area and along the northeasterly coast of South America. Most of these plans came to nothing, frustrated either by lack of equipment, lack of cooperation from the Navy, or lack of time – the command was dissolved before much could be done even on favorably considered plans. One project did, however, come close to realization. In the spring of 1943 it was proposed to survey the possibility of establishing antisubmarine coverage over the Atlantic Ocean in the general region of Polea, Natal, San Salvador, Ascension Island, Accra, and Dalmar.

This belt of ocean was little traversed by convoys, but frequently by independent vessels, and had been a fairly profitable resort for individual raiding U-boats. It was felt that this entire area could be covered if one or more antisubmarine squadrons, equipped with VLR (E) B-24's, were based at Natal, Brazil, or some other base in that vicinity, using Ascension Island and points on the West Coast of Africa as advance or alternate bases. AAF headquarters gave modified approval to the plan, suggesting in substance that it never does any harm to study possibilities of this sort provided definite commitments are not made. In this connection it should be observed that the Navy hoped by the fall of 1943 to have enough B-24's to handle the job, and in June 1943, it was anybody's guess who would ultimately control the SR aircraft engaged in antisubmarine warfare.

A project was begun, somewhat tentatively, in May, when on the 10th of that month two B-24D aircraft from the 8th Squadron were dispatched to Natal under the leadership of the squadron commander, Lt. Col. E. S. Beaks. This experimental detachment operated from Natal until the 27th, when it was moved, together with its ground echelon, to Ascension Island. During the following month, its strength increased to four B-34D's, one of which was normally based at Natal. Some confusion arose regarding its place in the command machinery of the South Atlantic, but finally it was placed under the Commander, South Atlantic Force, acting under the direction of the Commander in chief, US Atlantic Float. This arrangement was in accord with the procedure effective at the moment for control of all antisubmarine operations by the Joint Chiefs of Staff, with the Commander in Chief, US Fleet acting as the executive agent for this unified command. The detachment continued operations on this basis, with the official blessing of Vice Adm. Jonas H. Ingram, Commander, 4th Fleet, Recife, until its recall in August. During the period of its special duty, it flew 98 missions. Although it made few contacts with the enemy, it gathered considerable valuable information regarding German use of radar and radar detectors.

Nothing more came of the Antisubmarine Command's plans for the South Atlantic. Decisions concerning its fate, and that of antisubmarine activity generally, placed all such projects in abeyance.

8

THE NORTH ATLANTIC CONVOY ROUTE

In February and March of 1943, Admiral Doenitz made an all-out effort to render the North Atlantic convoy route unusable for Allied shipping. This attack was part of a general defensive strategy adopted to cut off or seriously harass the convoys bringing supplies to the invasion armies in Europe and Africa. And, as the North Atlantic convoys constituted the most important of these vital supply lines, the U-boat attack in the North Atlantic was the most concerted and desperate ever launched by the enemy. It therefore became essential to strengthen to the utmost the antisubmarine effort in that area; and to this end long-range air coverage was of paramount importance. So grave had the situation become by March, that President Roosevelt wrote on the 18th to the Chiefs of Staff, US Army and US Navy, asking how many B-24's could be operated at once from Newfoundland, Greenland, and Iceland, how many ACV's were on antisubmarine operations in the North Atlantic, and how soon the existing force of both could be brought to its maximum strength. If sufficient long-range bombers and ACV's were not promptly engaged in this battle of supply, the President warned, both HUSKY and BOLERO, as well as the security of Great Britain, might be seriously threatened.

In answer to the President's urgent message, the Chiefs of Staff vouchsafed the following information. Army, Navy, and Canadian air bases could support B-24's at the rate of 75 in Newfoundland, 40 in Iceland, and 6, for limited operations only, in Greenland. Plans to date did not, however, provide for numbers of this sort. For Newfoundland, the AAF had planned 12 B-24's by 1 May, and 18 by 1 June; and the US Navy had 12 which it hoped would be ready by June. Six Army Liberators had been earmarked for Greenland by 1 June. Iceland was to be left entirely to the RAF, whose Coastal Command had 8 B-24's in operation, 12 promised by 1 May, and 12 more by 1 June. In addition to the B-24's , 13 AAF Antisubmarine Command B-17's were ready for immediate shipment to Newfoundland to help cope with the convoy problem, although they were not so well suited to the work as the B-24's, owing to their shorter range. The Navy had an ACV in the area and planned to deploy two more in April. The British planned to put two ACV's on the convoy route. In short, with the U-boat war nearing its peak of intensity, the Allies were only able to put a handful of the vitally necessary VLR aircraft immediately into the battle. Adequate forces were planned, and diversions from other projects were suggested, but none could be made available before mid-summer.

This, then, was the desperate situation at the end of March. A few medium-range aircraft were being operated from Greenland and Iceland, and the 431st Bombardment Squadron (re-designated the 20th Antisubmarine Squadron on 8 February) had for some time been operating a few B-17's from Newfoundland. But the pressing problem still remained to provide long-range air cover for that middle portion of the North Atlantic route which had hitherto been beyond the range of the land-based aircraft available.

The problem had been recognized from the first, and the increasing intensity of the U-boat war in the North Atlantic stimulated discussion of it at the highest level. But it took most of the winter and spring of 1942-43 actually to equip Newfoundland with three antisubmarine squadrons from the AAF Antisubmarine Command; and by that time the climax of the struggle had already arrived. All that the AAFAC squadrons could do was to hasten, as best they could, the impending defeat of the Nazi submarine fleet.

A leading part in the discussion had been taken by the Canadian government. In December, Canada had been asked by Prime Minister Churchill whether it could supply the necessary bases, crews, and aircraft to undertake the task of providing air protection for the gap of approximately 250 nautical miles west of mid-ocean which was not being given air protection. Canada was able to supply the bases and crews, but could not provide the aircraft. Neither, at the moment, could the British. The Canadian Joint Staff then asked the AAF for aircraft. General Arnold disapproved the proposal on the ground that the AAF had no Liberators to spare. In March, the Atlantic Convoy Conference proposed that the AAF Antisubmarine Command operate three squadrons of B-24's from Newfoundland. By that time the situation in the North Atlantic had become so grave that every effort was made to equip and send these units as soon as possible. It had been estimated that by 1 July 1943 the AAF would have the necessary LR aircraft deployed as recommended by the Atlantic Convoy Conference, but General Arnold was concerned to implement the plan for Newfoundland immediately.

Meanwhile, the four B-17's of the 421st Bombardment Squadron, which had been operating for months under the Newfoundland Base Command as a reserve striking force, had also been carrying on antisubmarine patrol as a secondary duty under the control of Navy Task Force 24. They had been providing convoy coverage in a small square off the southeast corner of the island, in addition to the various odd jobs assigned to the unit. In order to increase the antisubmarine forces in the area, this squadron had been redesignated the 24th Antisubmarine Squadron and assigned antisubmarine patrol as its principal duty, under the Navy Task Force. In January, too, preliminary steps had been taken to extend long-range air coverage to Greenland. On the 35th the Director of Bombardment ordered the AAF Antisubmarine Command to conduct experimental operations from Greenland and to survey the facilities available there. And approximately a month later a report on the subject was submitted. Actual operations from Greenland had, however, to wait on the establishment of a regular B-24 patrol from Newfoundland, from which point all Greenland long-range operations were to be controlled.

Finally, on 13 March 1943, a detachment of the 25th Antisubmarine Wing left New York, under Col. Howard Moore, to establish a headquarters at St. John's, Newfoundland. On 3 April, this detached headquarters began operations in the control room of the combined headquarters of the Royal Canadian Navy and Royal Canadian Air Force. The 19th Antisubmarine Squadron also arrived late in March, and the 6th Antisubmarine Squadron a few weeks later. These squadrons were stationed at Gander Lake with the 20th Antisubmarine Squadron which had been in operation there for some time. A control room was set up for their use. The recently arrived squadrons, the 6th ad 19th, became operational on 5 April and 19 April, respectively. For the next three months the three squadrons conducted antisubmarine sweeps and convoy coverage from Gander under the supervision of the detachment headquarters. In early June, the 4th Antisubmarine Squadron joined the units at Gander and returned to the United States. Late in June 1943, when their services were no longer required in Newfoundland, the detachment headquarters (which on 13 June had been transferred on paper from the 25th Wing to the AAF Antisubmarine Command itself) was ordered to England, together with the units operating under it, the 4th, 6th, and 19th Antisubmarine Squadrons. These squadrons became part of the 479th Group. The 4th and 19th arrived in the United Kingdom in mid-July. The 6th, which had been left behind for a few weeks, assumed responsibility for AAFAC operations in Newfoundland in the absence of the detachment command post.

Operations originally were conducted under the immediate control of the detachment command post at St. John's and were subject, as usual, to coordination with the naval force in charge of that locality. On 30 April 1943, operational control of AAFAC units based in Newfoundland passed to Canada, in accordance with recommendations of the Atlantic Convoy Conference (par. 6, App. A, ACC-1) for an appropriate division of crew responsibility between the three countries most concerned with the North Atlantic antisubmarine war. It was a natural division, for, as far as air forces were concerned, the RCAF operated a majority of the antisubmarine aircraft in that area. The nature of this control remained general, however, and consisted of designating the missions to be performed, rather than prescribing how they were to be accomplished.

By the time the detachment headquarters began operations, the tactical situation had been pretty thoroughly surveyed by the Canadian agencies concerned. The great proportion of Allied convoys sailing to the United Kingdom had, because of fuel limitations, to pass through a relatively narrow bottleneck as they rounded Newfoundland and proceeded northeast along either the great circle or the northern routes. The enemy, recognizing this fact, apparently deployed his attack forces in such a way as to take maximum advantage of it. By March it was estimated by ROW intelligence that the Germans were setting up a patrol line of approximately 20 "informer" submarines, spaced about 20 miles apart along a line which cut across the convoy lanes in the bottleneck within the general area bounded by 51 degrees N. 49 degrees W., 47 degrees W., 50 degrees N., 40 degrees W., and 49 degrees N. 41 degrees W. This disposition of informer submarines afforded complete coverage of roughly 90 per cent of the North Atlantic trade convoys, and allowed the enemy to relay such information concerning these convoys as would be required for the main attacking forces, patrolling farther to northeast, to converge on each convoy with concentrated force and a significant economy of time, effort, and fuel.

According to this theory, then, the contact line became the most important target in the North Atlantic battle. To locate and attack its elements and so to put out the eyes of the U-boat fleet, became the primary objective of the antisubmarine forces operating from Newfoundland. During April and May it appeared that the Germans were extending this contact line farther to the south by adding probably 10 more submarines to cover the approaches to the southern route. Probably not more than 15 U-boats were deployed as an attack group, but, with the advantage of accurate advance intelligence, they were able to make every craft count in their attack on the convoys. The U-boat offensive in the North Atlantic reached its climax in a running attack on OWS-5 (22 April to 5 May 1943), during which 12 merchant vessels were torpedoed – 11 of them within less than 24 hours. The OWS-5 action, however, turned out also to be a turning point in the North Atlantic battle, for it was a costly victory, so costly that the enemy could ill afford many more such triumphs. Over 20 attacks were made on the U-boats by both surface craft and aircraft, resulting in 9 sunk or probably sunk and about 9 others damaged to some degree.

It was in this sort of battle that the AAFAC squadrons found themselves during April and May. Convoy coverage and offensive sweeps in broad areas ahead of convoys were their normal missions. In general the latter were the most productive of tangible results. For a few weeks, sightings were relatively frequent. The 24th Squadron, with only a few of its 7 B-17's (equipped with Mark II radar) available for patrol, flew 370 hours during March and made 7 sightings which resulted in 2 attacks, neither apparently damaging to the enemy. April proved to be a fairly productive month for the 3 squadrons. After the attack on OWS-5 early in May, the Germans began to withdraw their U-boat fleet gradually. As the waters off Newfoundland became correspondingly quiet, operations of the AAFAC squadrons consisted largely of escort missions. The following figures illustrate the changes in the situation, as far as the AAFAC squadrons were concerned, during the 2-month period:

Period	Escort Missions	Contacts	Sweeps	Contacts
2 April–2 May	454 hrs. 7 min.	1	588 hrs. 30 min.	10
3 May–31 May	1161 hrs. 53 min.	0	234 hrs. 56 min.	1
	1616 hrs. 5 min.	1	823 hrs. 25 min.	11

Few attacks resulted from the above listed contacts, and , of the 3 delivered, only 2 were assessed as damaging to the submarine. It must, of course, be remembered that the weather in the Newfoundland area permitted fewer efficient flying hours than in other areas of antisubmarine activity, with the exception of Greenland.

Part of the AAF Antisubmarine Command activity in the North Atlantic took place in Greenland. It had been announced by the high command on 16 March that a "Trans-Atlantic umbrella" consisting of Canadian, British, and American aircraft, was to be raised over the North Atlantic convoys in order to afford coverage for "every mile of the route from North America to Europe." Full responsibility for this broadening beneficence was to rest with the Canadian and British governments. Operations from Greenland and Iceland were necessary, in addition to these from Newfoundland, if this project were to be accomplished. The major part of the additional mid-ocean coverage had to come from Iceland, where the RAF and the US Navy normally maintained patrols. But it was felt that even sporadic long-range operations from Greenland would be enough to discourage the enemy in the vital mid-ocean gap. Accordingly, in spite of some of the most disheartening flying weather in the world (operations could be undertaken only 15 days in the month at the most suitable field in the country) it was decided to operate a small long-range force from Blue West One. Surveys of the area had been undertaken in February, but nothing could be done to provide the necessary long-range equipment and control personnel until the Detachment Headquarters had begun to function in Newfoundland.

Meanwhile, two AAF units, the 1st and 2d Provisional Bombardment Flights, were operating a few B-25D airplanes as an emergency striking force under the control of the Greenland Base Command. Although engaged in antisubmarine operations, the efforts of these flights were limited by the range of their aircraft and by lack of experience on the part of their crews. In addition to these small Army forces, the US Navy had a few RBY-5s and PY-1's at Blue West One under its Greenland Patrol Force which also undertook antisubmarine patrol. Such coordination of antisubmarine effort as was available came from the commander of this naval force. It had not been contemplated to use Blue West One for more than an advance operating base for planes based in Newfoundland. But it was not until close to the middle of May that anything was done even to use the Greenland base in that limited capacity or to open a control room there. By that time the crisis in the North Atlantic had already passed, and the enemy was withdrawing from the northern waters.

By June 1942 convoys were passing safely through lanes where a few weeks previously they had undergone the severest punishment. Admiral Doenitz had, in the face of increased Allied counterattacks and increased Allied activity in the Mediterranean, found it impossible to maintain his Newfoundland line. For a few weeks he had given everything he had to an all-or-nothing showdown in the North Atlantic. After the attack on OWB-5 he apparently decided to play for smaller and surer stakes. In his defeat, the green AAFAC squadrons had labored hard and not without effect, despite the few contacts obtained. There is no question that the increased long-range patrol that they were able to provide did much to reduce enemy mobility and to weaken enemy morale.

9

ANTISUBMARINE TACTICS AND ATTACK NARRATIVES

It was a strange type of warfare that the antisubmarine crews undertook, unlike any other in which the AAF had engaged. Hours of monotonous search were necessary. In areas of low U-boat density, some crews never saw a submarine, yet they had to maintain constant vigilance. Even in areas where the hunting was good, a crew might fly hundreds of hours without a sighting, then, in a matter of seconds, be required to go into action. For this kind of work crews had to be carefully trained to insure that no fumbling would mar an attack when the big moment finally came. Moreover, flying a thousand miles or more over open water requires export navigation. Radio communication must be reliable and the crew must be able to identify surface craft and aircraft with the utmost accuracy.

It is the attack itself that distinguishes antisubmarine flying most sharply from all other types. To be effective the depth bombs had to be laid within 20 feet of the submarine's pressure hull, and the aircraft was forced to drop close to the water, often to a scant 50 feet above the waves, in order to place them accurately. Each battle became a dual between the U-boat and the attacking plane, for the antisubmarine aircraft normally traveled alone. It might only last a few minutes, and during that time the crew had to function as a well-coached team, with all mechanical equipment in perfect condition.

It was hazardous work, too. Many crews had to face antiaircraft fire at close range or attack by enemy aircraft, often in considerable numbers, sent in to cover U-boat concentrations. Should the plane crash at sea, the crew knew it had few chances of surviving. The greatest danger to the aircraft came about during low-level attacks which made safety precautions generally useless; and under the best of conditions the plane would sink in a matter of seconds. Even if the crew survived a landing at sea it faced a disheartening prospect, for it would usually be hundreds of miles from land, dependent mainly on luck and the sometimes doubtful aid of its emergency equipment.

Experience had evolved certain basic principles for the conduct of antisubmarine operations by long-range aircraft. Patrol missions were planned in such a way that a given stretch of ocean would be covered in a more or less comprehensive pattern of flight, the crew depending when possible on its radar equipment to supplement the visual observation of its members. In this way a single plane could detect the presence of an enemy craft in a strip of water many miles wide. A radar-equipped plane might be expected to patrol effectively a 25-mile channel. Sweeps of this sort were normally routed toward areas in which U-boat concentrations were suspected, or in which individual raiders had been reported. Frequently the antisubmarine planes would be required to fly search sweeps in the neighborhood of convoys, the theory in this case being to prevent the enemy from closing in on its prey or even following it. Of course, if a submarine could be located and attacked, so much the better; but simply by forcing the enemy to dive and remain submerged for long periods, during which his speed would be greatly decreased, the patrolling aircraft could prevent a "wolf pack" from delivering a rapid and coordinated attack.

The big trick in this business of submarine hunting was to catch the submarine on the surface, or at least partially visible, and to deliver the attack before it had time to crash-dive. Analysis of attacks on submarines demonstrated that in approximately 35 per cent the submarines were still partly visible at the instant when the depth bombs were released and that in about 30 per cent of cases the enemy had disappeared less than 15 seconds. Attacks made after 15 seconds had small hope of success. Analysis further indicated that, in about two out of three instances, the submarine sighted the aircraft first.

It thus became an essential point of tactics to surprise the U-boat crew. Every possible use had to be made of camouflage and natural cover. Clouds, when available, provided by far the best cover; and by flying in and out of their bases, even by flying above formations of less than 5/10, the pilot was able to enjoy considerable concealment without materially reducing his chances of sighting submarines. Attacks from down sun, up moon path, and up to a dawn or dusk horizon proved effective. Camouflage of the plane itself also helped. Some were painted either Mediterranean blue or gray or olive drab on their upper half and off-white on their lower, with good effect.

Even with the best of cover and camouflage, the attack had to follow the sighting with the greatest possible speed. If the U-boat elected to dive, as it normally did, it could be out of sight in 30 seconds. If a maximum time of 45 seconds were allowed for the dive, and 15 more during which the submarine would be within range of depth bombs, the attack would have to be completed in 1 minute.

It was not always possible, therefore, to approach the U-boat at the best possible angle. If practicable, the pilot would cross his target at a small angle (15 to 45 degrees was considered best). In this way, without complicating his aim, he could considerably increase the probability that at least one depth bomb would do lethal damage. Normally a plane carrying only six depth bombs would drop them all on the first attack. If more were carried the second stick would be reserved for a subsequent attack. The bombs were spaced in such a way that at a normal height of 100 feet, the 325-pound charges would fall in a pattern of 50-foot intervals and those of 650 pounds at 70 feet intervals, thus making it possible for two of them to straddle the submarine and either tear its pressure hull seriously or even break it in two. Care had always to be exercised to attain the 100-foot level long enough before the attack to make the final approach in level flight. Nor was it wise to execute a run at too great speed, which simply increased the likelihood of error.

During the attack the aircraft gunners had to be prepared to bring machine-gun fire to bear on the U-boat, especially if the enemy crew showed signs of fighting back. Even under ordinary circumstances, it was considered advisable to fire along the hull of the submarine in the hope that penetration of its thin armor might do embarrassing damage to the fuel tanks or high-pressure air tanks.

If, as was usually the case, the aircraft crew could not be certain of the effect of their attack, or if they had not been able to make an attack at all, they were instructed to remain as long as possible in the area of the contact, or until relieved by other aircraft or by surface vessels summoned to the scene by radio. As long as a submarine is forced to remain submerged, the area to be searched is restricted to a minimum. In this way a concentration of forces in a cooperative killer hunt had a very good chance, if followed up persistently, of finally destroying the submarine. Sometimes, if the aircraft still had bombs, or had failed to release them at the initial contact, the pilot would drop a marker at the point where the submarine had disappeared, and resort to baiting tactics. After withdrawing some 20 miles, and staying away for 30 minutes to 1 hour, depending on his gas supply, he would return to the contact area on the chance that the enemy had surfaced again.

It was often difficult to determine the amount of damage inflicted, even by a well-executed attack, on an enemy submarine. Depth bombs themselves gave off a dirty oil residue which might easily be mistaken for the oily evidence of damage. Air bubbles appearing immediately after the depth bombs had detonated might only signify that the submarine was blowing or venting some tanks to adjust a temporary upset. Oil rising at this point might indicate damage to the external fuel tanks. If small air bubbles rose in a continuous stream, it was likely that the external connections to high-pressure air were damaged. This was annoying but not serious to the submarine. The U-boat might break surface momentarily after an attack and take up strange angles, stern or bow up. Yet even these signs might only mean a temporary loss of trim or control, rather than any serious damage. Large air bubbles that caused a disturbance on the surface and lasted for some time could be considered as evidence of trouble, and if accompanied by oil it meant that the enemy was in a desperate condition. In cases of this sort, if the submarine failed to reappear soon on the surface it would be considered sunk. Probably the only certain evidences of a "kill" were the appearance of survivors, or of bodies, or of a large amount of debris.

Most of the principles, outlined above, are exemplified, together with a number of unusual instances, in the following accounts of some of the more interesting attacks made by aircraft of the AAF Antisubmarine Command, which appeared in the monthly intelligence summary, published by that organization.

On 31 December 1943 the 1st Antisubmarine Squadron made its first important attack in the Bay of Biscay. It was a well-executed attack, making good use of the newly acquired radar equipment under adverse sea conditions. The attack was carried out at 1340 (GCF) by a B-24D, piloted by Capt. W.E. Thorne, while on patrol. An AFF contact was first made while the airplane was 8 miles distant at an altitude of 1000 feet. The pilot homed on the signal, on a course of 300 degrees, gradually reducing altitude, and sighted the submarine traveling on the surface at a speed of approximately 8 knots, course 320 degrees T. The submarine began its crash dive as Pilot Thorne started his run. Attacking from 4 points aft the starboard beam of the submarine, at a speed of 200 mph from 175-foot altitude, 9 depth bombs were dropped with a fuse setting of 25 feet and at a spacing of 10 feet. The stick straddled the hull just behind the conning tower. Three depth bombs fell to starboard, two over the hull, and the remainder to the port side. Approximately eighty-five .50-caliber rounds were fired at the disappearing hull and conning tower by the port ventral and tail gunners. The three depth bombs that fell to the starboard should have moved in and exploded directly under the storm of the U-boat, and the plume of the depth bombs contained a black streak believed to have been oil. At the point of attack was circled, an oil patch estimated to be 200 feet in diameter was observed, in the center of which numerous small bubbles were noticeable. A flame float was dropped, and the plane left the area on baiting procedure, returning 50 minutes later without seeing any further evidence of damage.

Tidewater Tillie was the B-24 in which 1st Lt. W.E. Sanford and his crew of the 2d Antisubmarine Squadron executed two attacks on enemy submarines which resulted in one probably sunk and one known sunk.

The first attack took place on 10 February about 800 miles west of St. Masairo while the squadron was operating out of Crest Britain. While patrolling at 300 feet at the base of a solid overcast, the left waist gunner sighted a U-boat on the surface 10 degrees off the port bow and about 4 miles away. A radar contact had been obtained in the same position a few seconds before, but owing to sea conditions, it had not been verified until the visual sighting was made.

When first observed, the conning tower was clearly seen, but, at the aircraft approached, it disappeared and about 40 feet of the storm was seen projecting out of the water at an angle of 20 degrees. As the aircraft attacked, no churning was visible from the screws of the apparently motionless U-boat. Six XI Torpex depth bombs, spaced for 19 feet, were released from 200 feet at 200 mph. The entire stick overshot: the first depth bomb was observed to explode about 20 feet to starboard of the submarine as the tail gunner fired 75 rounds at the exposed part of the hull.

As the pilot circled to port the U-boat settled back on an even keel with the conning tower visible and both decks awash. A second attack on the still motionless submarine was made with three more depth bombs. The tail gunner fired another 75 rounds and saw the first depth bomb explode on the port side, while a second exploded to starboard. The U-boat appeared to lift slightly, lurching with the force of the explosion, and then remained motionless on the surface.

While Lieutenant Sanford circled to make a third run, the sea was seen to be churned just astern of the U-boat, and the conning tower settled beneath the surface, without way, 15 seconds before the last three depth bombs were released. The detonations occurred about 200 feet ahead of the patch of disturbed water, but no plums resulted. Instead, a dome-shaped bubble appeared, followed by a large circular click of brown fluid which was described by the crew as definitely not depth-bomb residue. Nothing further was seen, and 30 minutes later the B-24 set course for base.

When first sighted, the U-boat apparently was attempting to dive at too steep an angle without sufficient way. This gave the pilot an opportunity to maneuver for two additional attacks which resulted, according to official assessment, in "probably sunk."

On 23 March, while operating out of a North African base, Lieutenant Sanford, again in Tidewater Tillie, made another attack in the vicinity of the Canary Islands which resulted in the complete destruction of the U-boat.

The B-24, camouflaged Mediterranean blue on its upper surfaces and cloud white underneath, was patrolling at 1300 feet, in and out of the cloud cover, when the co-pilot sighted a broad wake about 5 miles on the starboard beam. The pilot continued on his course into the next cloud, then made a 90-degree turn, immediately losing altitude. As the plane emerged from the cloud, the wake, still about 5 miles distant, was observed to be caused by a U-boat proceeding fully surfaced on course 180 degrees. Lieutenant Sanford decided to continue his run straight ahead and attack from the beam with the sun behind him rather than maneuver for a quartering or following attack. With the aircraft at 200 feet and making about 200 mph, the bombardier released four XXIX depth bombs spaced at 60 feet, allowing about 1000-feet range on the water.

The explosions enveloped the after portion of the U-boat which continued on its course for 11 seconds, then began to settle by the stern. The entire bow section from the conning tower forward was projecting out of the water and in about 1 minute slipped beneath the surface. Several survivors were observed clinging to debris which was strewn about the area, and a large oil slick developed. Half an hour later, as the plane was about to depart, a mass of brown, paint-like substance came up in the middle of the slick. This may have been rusty bilge oil discharged when the U-boat began to break up on the bottom.

The submarine was described as painted white with no markings. It had a streamlined conning tower and a very sharp bow. Three men were observed in the conning tower as the plane passed over. One of them tried to man the antiaircraft gun.

The attack was evidently a complete surprise and was achieved by a combination of effective camouflage, clever use of cloud cover, attacking out of the sun, and accurate bombing.

On 20 February 1945 a B-24 of the 1st Antisubmarine Squadron, piloted by Lt. W.S. Johnson, was on patrol over the Bay of Biscay in the area 49 degrees 30'W., some 600 miles from base. It was flying at 1600 feet through broken clouds that extended down to about 700 feet when the navigator in the nose sighted the broad wake of a fully surfaced U-boat about 3 miles away. The pilot immediately dived to attack, entering the clouds and emerging when about 1 mile distant from the U-boat.

Apparently the aircraft had not been spotted since the U-boat was still on the surface. The B-24 went in with its bow gun raking the conning tower. Six depth bombs spaced for 26 feet were dropped from 200 feet and were seen to straddle the hull just aft of the bow. The force of the explosions lifted the bow, and, as the plums fell away, another explosion was seen on the port side in the vicinity of the conning tower. This explosion caused no plume but a boiling plume appeared on the water. Fifteen seconds later the conning tower disappeared without any noticeable headway, and a bluish-gray oil slick about 400 feet long formed on the water. Some small bubbles were seen rising in the center of the slick, and the navigator reported seeing a greenish patch, possibly air, rising to the surface.

Baiting tactics were employed but nothing further was seen. Ninety minutes after the attack the aircraft left the area and returned to base. This attack probably resulted in severe damage.

Early in March 1943 there took place in the Caribbean a good example of a killer hunt in a convoy area. Early on the evening of 3 March, while returning from a convoy escort mission in the Trinidad area, the 9th Anti-submarine Squadron picked up a good instrument contact at 17 miles. Haze and darkness restricted visibility to less than 1 mile, so the pilot had to home on the target, increasing speed and losing altitude at the same time. From three-quarters of a mile a wake was sighted and as the plane passed over at 400 feet it was identified as a fully surfaced submarine on course 330 degrees, speed 12 knots. While the target remained on the radar screen the pilot immediately turned and lost more altitude. The attack was made 90 degrees to the course of the submarine which was still visible when the bombs were released. Two Mark XXIX and two Mark XVII depth bombs were released from 100 feet and were seen to enter the water about 50 feet ahead of the swirl. Apparently the U-boat had just submerged as the bombs hit. All charges were observed to explode directly in the track of the submarine, but because of darkness no evidence of damage could be seen.

Edinburgh Field dispatched another P-18B as soon as the message from the attacking plane was received. About 2 hours later this plane obtained an initial radar indication about 8 miles distant at 45 degrees to starboard in a position 12 miles northeast of the scene of the first attack. The pilot approached the target and, when 1 mile away, altitude 200 feet, he turned on his landing lights. The submarine immediately opened fire with two guns, one firing slightly higher than the other. Tracer bullets were plainly seen as the pilot banked steeply to the right, turned off the landing lights and drew out of range. The P-18B returned and positively identified it as an enemy submarine on course 300 degrees making about 15 knots. The U-boat crash-dived immediately, making it impossible for the plane to make a second run.

A square search of the area was begun and 2 hours later a radar contact was made at 11 miles, bearing 60 degrees to port. The plane homed on the target, dropping to 200 feet, and made three passes over the fully surfaced submarine in an attempt to line up on the target. On the fourth pass, the submarine was still proceeding on the surface at 15 knots, course 75 degrees. Two Mark XXIX and two Mark XVII, spaced for 20 feet, were seen to enter the water, straddling the submarine between the conning tower and stern. At least three explosions were observed; the other bomb may have hit the U-boat, or hit so close to it that the explosion was not seen. Following the attack the area was searched for 30 minutes for evidence of damage but nothing could be seen due to darkness.

These two attacks, delivered under difficult circumstances, probably saved the convoy from an attack and caused possible damage to the enemy submarine. When the submarine was sighted again at 2110 by the P-18B which relieved the original plane, its course of 300 degrees and speed 15 knots indicated that the submarine was persisting in its original intent. The fact that it opened fire on the plane and failed to submerge while the plane made four passes is not positive indication that the first attack resulted in damage sufficient to prohibit the prompt execution of a crash dive. However, it appears very probable that the net result of the two attacks was sufficient damage to hinder the enemy greatly in his efforts to evade the extensive search by airplane and surface craft which ensued.

Six days later a Navy PBY was hunting 500 miles east of these attacks for a possible crippled U-boat limping its way back home. From 4500 feet, a fully surfaced submarine was sighted about 3 miles distant on a course of 93 degrees and making 8 knots. Making good use of cloud cover, the aircraft maneuvered to attack out of the sun. Diving to 75 feet, four Mark XVII depth bombs were dropped in salvo, landing alongside the hull about 10 to

15 feet away. As the bombs exploded the submarine appeared to rise out of the water, then split in two at the center. Debris, smoke, and water were thrown 50 feet in the air. At least 11 survivors were seen in the water.

Celebrating the arrival of the 6th Antisubmarine Squadron in Newfoundland, Lt. E.J. Dudeck in a B-34D made an excellent attack on 19 April 1943. The B-24D, camouflaged white, was flying on a course of 147 degrees W. through weather conditions that were fair for submarine hunting, with the sun obscured by low stratus clouds at 1000 feet and with visibility varying up to 2 miles. At 1443Z, while Lieutenant Dudeck was taking full advantage of cloud cover, a submarine was sighted at 353 degrees about half a mile distant, proceeding on a course of 10 degrees N., at about 2 knots.

At the moment of sighting the U-boat, the airplane crew was engaged in transferring fuel, and fact action was necessary since the enemy apparently had already spotted the plane and started to dive. The pilot immediately pushed the plane into a dive for the attack while the crew scrambled to their stations. The conning tower disappeared 10 seconds after the original sighting, but six Mark XVII depth bombs, spaced at 35 feet with 25-feet depth settings, were released 5 seconds later, while 10 to 15 feet of the diving U-boat's stern were still visible. The U-boat appeared to be a dirty grey color, about 200 feet long, with a 3-inch gun mounted forward of the conning tower.

The pilot led the visible stern of the U-boat by about 150 feet and while the first depth bomb was about 35 feet short and the fourth, fifth and sixth were over, the second and third appeared to straddle each side of the U-boat slightly ahead of the conning tower. A large yellowish green oil slick was observed immediately after the attack and air bubbles about 1 foot in diameter appeared 50 feet ahead of the last-observed position of the stern. The plane remained in the vicinity for 1 hour and 45 minutes and a B-17 later searched the area for 3 hours. No further evidence of damage appeared.

The attack, executed accurately in a minimum of time, appears to have been carried out in a superior manner. While evidence of a definite kill was lacking, the probabilities favored at least severe damage to the U-boat.

On 2 May 1943, Capt. H. J. Larson and his crew in a B-17 of the 19th Antisubmarine Squadron had a field day off the coast of Newfoundland.

They appear to have happened upon one of those U-oat packs by means of which the Germans were currently attempting to close the North Atlantic convoy route. A period of poor weather had restricted flying for several days previous, and even on this day haze, light rain, and fog prevented all the scheduled missions from taking off. Another result of the protracted low-pressure area which hung offshore was to draw in the U-boat pack which usually patrolled from 500 to 600 miles off Newfoundland to within 300 miles. A convoy, OWS-3, was in the vicinity of Greenland at this time and proceeding on a southerly course for Halifax. Apparently the submarines were working into position to intercept it. Captain Larson was dispatched to sweep an area about 300 miles ahead of the convoy.

In the course of the afternoon three U-boats were sighted and attacked by this plane. The first contact was obtained at 1945Z when an enemy craft was seen 3 miles away proceeding with decks awash. The submarine appeared to be of the 740-ton type with deck guns fore and aft and a stream-lined conning tower 13 to 15 feet long. It was painted solid black. The air-craft attacked on a course of approximately 45 degrees to the U-boat, drop-ping four Mark XVII depth bombs from 50 feet spaced at 20 feet. The top of the conning tower was still visible at the time of release. All the bombs were seen to detonate. With respect to the conning tower the first explosion was estimated about 40 feet short, the second 10 feet short, the third a direct hit, and the fourth about 10 feet over. As the bombs exploded, the conning tower appeared to lift about 3 feet and then settled under. Tracers from the nose and top turret were seen to hit in the conning tower area. After the attack, a heavy black oil slick 500 feet in diameter was seen.

Two hours later a conning tower was sighted 3 miles away, in a position about 50 miles from the first contact. This U-boat, which was also painted black, appeared to be of the 500-ton type with a small conning tower and a deck gun forward. The aircraft attacked on a course of 180 degrees to the U-boat with .50-caliber machine guns only, since all depth bombs had been expanded in the first attack. As theB-17 circled, the U-boat was seen to sub-merge in a normal dive.

A half hour later another submarine was sighted in the same area. It was not moving and the deck was dry as if it had been surfaced for some time. A high, rust-colored conning tower and one deck gun forward was observed.

As the aircraft went in to attack, six men were seen on deck; one, at the gun, may have fired upon the plane. At least two men were left in the conning tower when the U-boat crash-dived. One appeared to be hit by the fire from the .50- and .30-caliber machine guns.

In all three attacks the aircraft was patrolling at about 200 feet. Visibility varied between 3 and 6 miles. All contacts were first picked up on special equipment which was used continuously, and without which the crew believed the sightings could not have been made. It is to be regretted that the limited bomb load of the B-17 prevented more serious damage to the enemy.

On 19 June 1943 a B-24D of the 2d Antisubmarine Squadron, piloted by Capt. William Sanford, took off from Port Lyautey on convoy escort duty in the early morning hours. At 0623, with visibility still restricted by darkness, at an altitude of 1200 feet, the radar operator reported two indications at 20 to 302 miles, in a position about 10 miles behind the convoy. Captain Sanford lost altitude as he neared the area and opened the bomb bay doors, but the contact was lost. Turning to starboard, he climbed again to 1500 feet, and soon another indication was picked up to the starboard at 7 miles.

As the plane started its run, it let down to 400 feet, and from a distance of 1 mile sighted a 517-ton German U-boat with decks awash, making a speed of 12 to 15 knots on a course of 90 degrees. The submarine immediately opened fire on the plane with cannon and machine guns, to which the plane's navigator replied with 25 rounds from the nose gun, scoring hits on the deck and conning tower. The U-boat's fire ceased when the B-24 came within 100 yards, but the navigator fired another burst for good measure.

The U-boat was still on the surface, making no attempt to crash-dive, when the bombardier released six Mark 47 350-pound depth bombs, with a 60-foot spacing and 25-foot setting. The plane, which was flying at 100 feet, attacked from the starboard beam at an angle of 100 degrees to the course of the submarine. The tail and left waist-gunners reported the explosions were seen 10 to 20 feet ahead of the U-boat's stern with numbers 3 and 4 straddling the hull. The force of the explosions lifted 5 feet of the submarine's stern out of the water at a 30 degree to 40 degree angle. As the plane passed over, the U-boat's guns fired again, but less heavily this time; and a few seconds later the submarine slid under the surface, bow first. The

German gun crew was evidently left in the water, for they were still firing when the U-boat submerged. The screws were apparently damaged or destroyed in the attack, for there was no sign of churning when the stern sank. A large piece of debris was left on the surface.

Having dropped a flame float and circled to port, the plane made a second attack up the U-boat's track 40 seconds later. This time the remaining two depth bombs were released, guiding on the flame float, and the debris left from the first attack was scattered by the explosion. An oil slick 300 to 400 feet long and 20 feet wide was seen, but darkness obscured the scene, making observation of further results impossible. The B-24 reported to the convoy and after resurveying the area resumed its patrol.

This attack was assessed as resulting in "probably slight damage." It was one of the few successful night attacks made by the Antisubmarine Command.

On 7 July an airplane of the 1st Antisubmarine Squadron, piloted by Lt. T. A. Isley, was out hunting about 230 miles southwest of Lisbon with ceiling and visibility unlimited and scattered clouds at 1500 feet. The aircraft was flying at 170 mph in and out of the base of the clouds, when a radar contact was obtained at a distance of 15 miles. Lieutenant Isley immediately altered course and a fully surfaced U-boat was sighted at 8 miles distance, making 8 to 9 knots on a course of 20 degrees true. As the aircraft let down still about 4 miles away, the U-boat was observed crash-diving. It was obvious that an attack could not be made while the U-boat was still on the surface, with the result that careful judgment was required if the attack was to be a success.

Lieutenant Isley estimated that fully 10 seconds had elapsed since the conning tower disappeared before six Mark 47 depth bombs were released by interval meter. The bombs were spaced at 80 feet, fused at 25 feet, and released from 200 feet. The explosions straddled the advance track of the U-boat approximately 200 feet ahead of the swirl at a target angle of 260 degrees. This angle of attack afforded a broad coverage of the submerged course of the U-boat, and soon indications of results appeared. About 45 seconds after the explosions, a large, black oil bubble rose to the surface, continued to erupt oil for 3 minutes, and spread over an extensive area 600 to 700 feet in diameter. Lieutenant Isley remained in the area for 40 minutes after the attack but observed no further evidence of damage. Commich considered this submarine to be severely damaged.

On the same day and in the same general area, another aircraft of the 1st Antisubmarine Squadron, while patrolling at 3000 feet, obtained a radar contact at 7 miles. Almost simultaneously, Lt. W. S. McDonnell, the pilot, sighted a fully surfaced 517-ton U-boat proceeding northwesterly at about 8 knots. He immediately altered his course to starboard and let down to make the attack.

As he approached, the U-boat swung off to starboard and opened fire from the conning tower with its gun. The pilot pressed the attack despite the AA fire, and as the aircraft passed over the U-boat from the port side at a target angle of approximately 270 degrees, 7 Mark 47 depth bombs were released by the bombardier. Both the navigator and the top turret gunner returned the fire of the U-boat, strafing the conning tower and the deck. The explosions of the bombs straddled the target, which was seen to break in two at the conning tower. Members of the air crew then observed the after section of the U-boat rise 10 or 12 feet into the air, roll to starboard, then settle and sink with no forward motion.

As the aircraft was attacking, a 20-millimeter shell from the U-boat struck the top center panel of the nose. Several members of the crew were seriously injured by the burst, including the navigator, bombardier, radio operator, and assistant radio operator. In addition, the aircraft itself suffered minor damage, as the shell knocked out the radio compass, the hydraulic system, and most of the engine instruments. With the plane damaged and most of the crew injured, Lieutenant McDonnell headed for home.

Although Lieutenant McDonnell was not able to remain in the area to observe further results, photographic evidence indicated a perfect straddle, and the testimony of the crew suggests that the U-boat was destroyed.

The following day, 8 July, another attack was made by a plane of the 2d Antisubmarine Squadron, about 150 miles north of the previous day's action. The aircraft, piloted by Lt. J. E. Darden, was flying at 3000 feet through a broken overcast when radar contact was made on a U-boat off to starboard and 18 miles distant. Approaching through the base of the clouds, Lieutenant Darden, planned the attack so that he would come down out of the sun in a steep dive. The maneuver worked out according to plan. Upon sighting the U-boat ahead 8 miles distant, proceeding at 13 knots in a south-easterly direction, the plane dove steeply, leveled off, and passed over the submarine at an altitude of 50 feet. The target angle was 370 degrees and four Mark 37 650-pound depth bombs were observed to straddle the U-boat between the bow and the conning tower. The tail gunner observed the surfaced U-boat running directly into the center of the explosion.

This attack had not been delivered without opposition; once again, the U-boat commander elected to remain on the surface and defend himself with AA fire. From 300 yards on in, the B-24D was under fire, suggesting that the use of the sun almost achieved a complete surprise attack. As the aircraft passed over, however, one burst struck the starboard side of the nose, but caused only minor damage. Fire was returned during the attack by the top turret, nose, and tail guns. Lieutenant Darden made a sharp climbing turn to port after delivering the first attack, and prepared for another run. The enemy craft was now circling, out of control, in a series of tight turns, gradually losing speed and trailing a long stream of brown oil. A large cloud of dark smoke poured from a point directly abaft the conning tower, and, in addition, the stern was submerged completely with the bow rising higher out of the water.

The aircraft returned for a second attack at a 50-foot altitude and a target angle of 80 degrees. On this occasion the U-boat's AA fire was more effective, scoring numerous hits on the wing, fuselage, and bomb bay, cutting the hydraulic and fuel lines and damaging the radio equipment and the command radio transmitter. Unfortunately, the damage to the bomb bay doors now made it impossible to release the additional two depth bombs as the aircraft passed over on this run. Machine-gun fire from the plane, however, continued to make the U-boat, which now had slowed to two or three knots, continuing tight turns and gradually losing all forward motion. Finally it disappeared, stern first, settling slowly with no churning or other surface indications. There were still two depth bombs aboard, however, and the crew prepared for a third attack.

The bombardier, Lt. C. J. Froccaro, succeeded in opening the doors of the bomb bay despite the damage, and two more Mark 37's were dropped upon the settling U-boat, which was silhouetted beneath the surface. The explosions of these bombs straddled the conning tower and were accompanied by a third blast of greater intensity. This third plume appeared to be higher than normal, thick and dark in color.

This series of attacks had consumed approximately 20 minutes. It was skillfully executed, beginning with the use of the sun and cloud cover, and ending with a successful release of the remaining two depth bombs. Heavy and accurate enemy AA fire did not deter the pilot from completing very accurate runs over the target, and the bombardier released the bombs in both instances with superior skill. The results of the attack were visible on the surface, for heavy oil spread over the entire area. Owing to the damage sustained, and to minor injuries suffered by one crew member, the pilot was unable to remain in the vicinity to observe further indications of success.

On the 9th of July a B-24 of the 2d Squadron attacked and probably destroyed a submarine. The plane was flying at 3200 feet, taking advantage of 3/10 cloud cover when Lieutenant Gerhart, the bombardier, sighted a U-boat apparently just surfacing about 4 miles dead ahead. It was the 517-ton type, camouflaged slate gray.

Lt. T. E. Kuenning, the pilot, immediately put the aircraft into a dive, leveling off at 50 feet. Six Mark XI 250-poung Torpex-filled depth bombs were released, straddling the bow with one short and five over. The explosions occurred just aft of the conning tower. No enemy fire was encountered. No one was seen on deck, confirming the supposition that the submarine may have been surprised just as it surfaced.

The pilot circled immediately and, as the spray subsided, came in again for a second attack on the still surfaced U-boat. This attack was almost head-on, and two more Mark XI were released, exploding aft of the conning tower on the port side as the enemy craft appeared to be attempting a crash dive. As the plane climbed away to port, six crew members saw the bow rise 1q5 feet out of the water at an angle of 45 degrees; then the hull slid backwards, sinking stern first. The entire action was over in 2 minutes.

A very unusual attack in which radar played a very important role occurred on the 12th of July about 200 miles northwest of Lisbon. Lt. E. Salem, the pilot, was flying at 5600 feet over a solid overcast, using radar continuously, when a contact was obtained about 13 miles dead astern. The pilot turned and descended through the overcast on instruments at 240 mph, constantly receiving headings from the radar operator.

The B-24D finally broke through at 200 feet, and a surfaced U-boat was sighted on the starboard bow 1 mile away. Immediately the navigator and top turret gunner opened fire and tracers were seen to rake the entire conning tower area. No enemy personnel was seen, but lookouts must have been present. Seven Mark XI 250-pound Torpex-filled depth bombs were released while the aircraft was still in a slight dive. Because of the angle at the time of release, the spacing of the bombs was somewhat shortened, but in this case the shorter spacing probably resulted in maximum effectiveness, owing to the accuracy with which the bombs were released.

The crew saw the explosions straddle the submarine, and , as the pilot made a vertical turn at 100 feet, the U-boat broke in two and sank. The entire area was covered with oil, and large bubbles appeared for several minutes. While Lieutenant Salem continued to circle, low and very tightly because of the limited ceiling and restricted visibility, 15 survivors were counted in the water. The air crew dropped a dinghy and smoke flares. As the plane departed seven survivors were still seen in the water.

This remarkable attack demonstrated what skillful use of radar equipment, coupled with the alertness and audacity of the pilot and crew, could do, even in the face of adverse weather conditions.

On 28 July an excellent example of a cooperative attack took place. On that date, Lt. A. J. Hammer of the 4th Squadron had set a course to return to base from the vicinity north of Cape Finisterre. Flying at 4000 feet and in light clouds on a course of 30 degrees, the B-24D was approximately 150 miles north of the Cape when a fully surfaced U-boat was sighted 5 miles off to starboard. The U-boat, which appeared to be of the 740-ton type and well camouflaged, was proceeding at 10 knots on a course of 250 degrees.

Lieutenant Hammer immediately altered his course to prepare to attack out of the sun which was now down in the west. The U-boat had altered its course 90 degrees to starboard shortly after it was sighted, and now was on a northwesterly course, continually zigzagging. As the aircraft closed in to attack, the U-boat opened fire at a range of 2 ½ miles with two guns abaft the conning tower, but, despite the intense flak, no hits were scored upon the Liberator on this run. At 1000 yards, the two top turret guns and nose gun opened accurate fire on the U-boat, registering hits all along the deck, knocking two men overboard, and temporarily silencing all AA fire.

From an altitude of 100 feet the bombardier released 8 Mark XI Torpex depth bombs, spaced at 60 feet, of which 5 fell short and 3 just beyond the conning tower, thus securing an accurate straddle at a target angle of approximately 270 degrees. The pilot circled to port to prepare for a second attack, and this time the bombardier released 4 Mark XI bombs spaced at 100 feet from an altitude of 50 feet and at a target angle of 90 degrees. The U-boat was still on the surface and all 4 of the depth bombs fell short, the last one falling only 5 feet from the hull. Unfortunately, during this second run, the turret guns jammed and the nose gun had exhausted its ammunition, which left no defense against the renewed AA fire of the U-boat. The No. 1 engine of the Liberator was completely knocked out, and additional damage was suffered in the tail assembly as a result of the intense AA fire.

At this point a second Liberator appeared on the scene, attracted by the depth-bomb plumes of the original attack, and before the U-boat could submerge, the new arrival, a Coastal Command B-24, commanded by Flight Officer Sweeney, was able to deliver a third attack. Seven more Torpex depth bombs straddled the U-boat, with the third one falling alongside the conning tower. Before the plumes had entirely subsided, the enemy craft had disappeared, but immediately surfaced on an even keel, then submerged once more with bow projecting high out of the water. Once again an attack was delivered by the second aircraft, and the U-boat disappeared. Two extensive oil patches spread over the sea, large air bubbles rose to the surface, and 10 men in life jackets were observed swimming amid the debris and oil. During the run in, the second Liberator had been hit in the No. 4 engine which was set afire, but fortunately both aircraft reached their bases safely. Despite damage to Lieutenant Hammer's aircraft, his crew suffered no injuries. This attack was assessed as a definite kill.

A B-24D of the 4th Antisubmarine Squadron attacked and sank an enemy submarine on 2 August 1943. The aircraft was patrolling at 2500 feet on top of scattered clouds about 400 miles west of St. Nazaire when a radar contact was obtained indicating a target 20 miles distant and 50 degrees to starboard. Lt. J. L. Hamilton, the pilot, changed course and 5 minutes later the co-pilot, Lt. R. C. Schmidt, sighted a large wake about 30 degrees to starboard and approximately 10miles away. As the aircraft et down from out of the sun, a surfaced U-boat was sighted, apparently homebound on a course of 30 degrees.

When the B-24D was 1 mile away the submarine opened fire with light flair, scoring one hit on the left wheel, but most of the firing was very inaccurate. The aircraft's top turret opened fire at 1500 yards distance, the front guns began at 500 yards, and both registered hits all along the U-boat decks. Antiaircraft shelling subsided as the plane made its final run at a target angle of 90 degrees.

From an altitude of 50 feet the bombardier intended to drop 8 depth bombs, but actually a train of 12 Torpex Mark XI depth bombs were released. The tail gunner observed the charges straddling the U-boat. The American A-1 bombsight was used but the plane's interval meter, previously known to be unreliable, was not used on order of the squadron commander. The 12 depth charges were released by toggle and the crew estimated their spacing at 50 feet. As the plumes subsided, the tail gunner observed the entire U-boat lifted out of the water. It quickly settled by the stern as the bow raised to an angle of 30 degrees. The submarine continued to sink stern first and disappeared 10 seconds after the depth bombs were dropped.

After the aircraft had circled to port, at least 15 men were seen in the water. White and yellow pieces of wood and a large amount of oil were floating on the surface. The B-24D dropped two marine markers, and 5 minutes later tossed out a rubber dinghy to the survivors. Five men were seen to climb aboard the raft.

This attack is an excellent example of radar and visual search, followed by a clever approach out of the sun. This tactic probably contributed to the aircraft's relative safety in the face of antiaircraft fire.

It has been pointed out in other parts of this study that the AAF Antisubmarine Command units operating in the Eastern Atlantic frequently had to give as much attention to enemy aircraft as they did to enemy submarines. No account of their activities would complete without at least an example of the frequently violent action involved in these engagements. Most of the aircraft encountered were medium JU-88's, which were being employed for the primary purpose of intercepting antisubmarine planes. Later in the summer of 1943, the Germans also sent their heavy, four-engine FW-200's into the fight. The primary mission of these bombers was antishipping strikes for which their long range (they often operated as far as 700 miles from their bases) made them ideally suited. But their long range also allowed them to intercept the B-24's when the latter had flown far beyond the range (seldom over 300 miles) of the JU-88. These heavy bombers gave the AAFAC crews virtually their only action in August when the submarines themselves had acknowledged their defeat and were staying carefully out of range of the B-24's.

It was with the FW-200's that probably the most dramatic of the many air engagements took place. On the 17th of August a B-24D of the 1st Anti-submarine Squadron was on convoy coverage 300 miles west of Lisbon, when two Focke-Wulf 200's were sighted. The B-24D was flying at 1500 feet below an overcast when it received a radar contact, indicating a target at 12 to 15 miles, 30 degrees left. After turning towards the target, a second blip was obtained at 8 miles, 5 degrees left. The aircraft climbed to 2300 feet and homed on the target. At 4 miles, it descended through the overcast to 1000 feet. Finally, at a distance of 1 mile, two FW-200's were sighted, just beginning a parallel bombing run on the convoy.

The nearest FW fired a sighting burst at the approaching B-24 and banked to the left. Captain Maxwell, the pilot, followed on its tail and slightly above. The other FW closed in from astern. The three planes were in line at this point and all opened fire. The fire from the enemy aircraft appeared to be from 20-millimeter cannon. The first German aircraft dived to 50 feet, with the B-24 and second FW following. After 1 minute of combat, Nos. 3 and 4 engines of the B-24 were out. Large holes were seen in the wing and fuselage and the right wing was ablaze. Nevertheless, the B-24 continued to gain on the first FW, scoring many hits on the inner wing, fuse-lage, and port engines of the leading FW. As the B-24 passed over this air-craft, it was seen to break into flames and crash into the sea.

Meantime, the tail gunner and right waist gunner had been returning the fire of the trailing Nazi aircraft, and not the top turret gunner turned around to join in that engagement. The B-24, however, was almost out of control and the crew took up ditching stations immediately. There was no time for ditching orders. Owing to cut hydraulic lines, the bombardier was unable to release the depth bombs, but the navigator used the emergency release and jettisoned the bombs a minute before ditching.

The right wing of the B-24D hit the water first. The plane skidded sideways with little shock, making about a 180 degree turn. On the second impact, the aircraft broke in three pieces at the trailing edges of the wings and at the waist windows. The nose section floated for 1 ½ minutes, but the other two sections sank almost immediately. The pilot and co-pilot escaped through the broken windshield, the navigator and radio operator through the escape hatch. Two others of the crew escaped through a break in the top of the fuselage near the waist windows, while the tail gunner went through the top of the tail turret which had partially broken off.

Two life rafts were then released and seven survivors, all of whom were slightly wounded with shrapnel, climbed aboard. Three men were lost including the radar operator, who, it is believed, was pinned to his seat by the radar set.

Meanwhile, the second FW could still be seen by the crew mushing along at 50 feet with No. 3 engine out and tail heavy. In 15 minutes, the crew members were picked up by one of the escort vessels from the convoy. Survivors from the first Focke-Wulf were also rescued a short time later. Seamen from two of the naval vessels said that they saw the second German bomber crash. At the same time, a radar indication on the screen of the escort leader disappeared at about 8 miles, tending to confirm the destruction of the second German plane.

It is to be noted that in this and other encounters with FW-200's, 20-millimeter fire was experienced from both the front and rear of the "bathtub." The B-24D, however, appeared to be approximately 20 miles per hour faster, even with a full bomb load, and more maneuverable than its adversary.

Throughout the sharpest of the fighting, whether with enemy aircraft or in attacks on submarines, the B-24 proved to be by far the best land-based aircraft for the job, especially in its modified form (B-24D). Indeed, the modified Liberator had no rival anywhere in the antisubmarine forces, except in the carrier-based planes developed by the U.S. Navy and employed effectively during and after the summer of 1943.

It is a pity that the AAF Antisubmarine Command was unable to profit more fully from the technical research undertaken in the field of antisubmarine warfare. No agency appreciated more keenly the potential value of improved devices and weapons; and it did all in its power to stimulate development along lines suggested by experience in that highly specialized kind of combat. The story of its efforts in this direction will be told in Chapter IV. At this point it will be enough simply to state certain general facts. First, it must be remembered that the Command did profit to some extent from the research done prior to its activation and during the course of its career. Most useful of all antisubmarine aids was radar, which, in the form of the SCR-517 type, did yeoman service during 1943 and accounted for many contacts that might not otherwise have been made. Improved, though by no means ideal, low-level bomb sights were in irregular use by the summer of 1943. And by that time also the modified B-24D, with its greatly increased forward firing power, was ready for use. Early in 1943, more dependable bombing was made possible by the adoption of the flat-nosed depth bomb. The absolute altimeter was completed in time for it to be used effectively by this command, with the result that safer and more accurate bombing runs could be made at low altitudes. Most of the other projects, and their number was legion, were not completed in time to be of any use to the AAF Antisubmarine Command. Great things were expected of the new detection devices, especially the magnetic airborne detector and the radio sonic buoy. And in the field of lethal weapons, rocket projectiles and retro bombing devices promised greatly increased precision in antisubmarine attacks. But as far as the command was concerned, their value remained largely potential. Indeed, the greatest tactical progress made by the command appears to have come about as a result simply of increased experience in the operation of those devices and techniques already in use when the command took over, or developed shortly thereafter.

10

SUMMARY AND RESULTS OF AAF ANTISUBMARINE COMMAND OPERATIONS

It is hard to find an adequate criterion for measuring the results of the Army Air Forces antisubmarine operations. In addition to locating and destroying hostile submarines, the mission of the AAF Antisubmarine Command included "assisting the Navy in the protection of friendly shipping." In the 8-month period from January to August 1943, purely defensive escort missions totaled 43,264 hours. Even these figures do not fully reflect the extent of the effort in protecting friendly shipping, for most of the flying in the western Atlantic was of a purely defensive nature. Of the total operational hours flown by the command, 56 per cent were accounted for by squadrons based on the western side of the ocean, yet this primarily defensive flying yielded only 29 per cent of the attacks. Although it is obviously impossible to estimate the number of ships that may have been saved by this great defensive effort, the presumption is that it was large.

The following table will give some idea not only of the total activity of the AAF Antisubmarine Command, but that of the I Bomber Command as well:

	Operational Combat Hours	Total Attacks
I Bomber Command	59,248	81
Antisubmarine Command		
Eastern Atlantic	12,215*	37
Western Atlantic	75,879*	15
Totals	147,342	133

*Through September 1943.
**Two of these kills were made with the help of RAF aircraft.

A—Sunk	6
B – Probably sunk	4
C – Probably severely damaged to the extent that sub failed to reach port	1
D – Probably severely damaged	11
E – Probably slightly damaged	15
Totals	37

Key to other assessments: F—insufficient evidence of damage; G—no damage; H—insufficient evidence of presence of submarines; I—non-submarine; J—insufficient data for analysis or inconclusive.

Thus a total of at least 37 enemy submarines suffered from attacks by aircraft of the command and its predecessor. Of these, probably 11 failed to reach port at a cost to the enemy of some $55,000,000 to $75,000,000 and the lives of more than 500 men. Eleven others were severely damaged and 15 slightly damaged. The British had a rule of thumb that about 30 per cent of the "severely damaged" and 5 per cent of the "slightly damaged" usually fail to reach port. If such a measure were applied to the above figures, it would indicate that a total of 15 U-boats were destroyed. There is no way of telling how much inconvenience was caused by the attacks of lower assessment, but it would be reasonable to suppose that they failed in most instances to simplify the task of the U-boat commander.

In this connection the probable effect of aircraft attacks on the U-boat crews must be recognized. No submarine crew likes to make emergency crash dives since there is always the chance that some mistake will be made, some valve left open. Furthermore, the crews know that crash dives use up valuable electricity and if repeated too often will leave the craft in a vulnerable position. Frequent air patrols, insofar as they make frequent crash dives necessary, had a gradually corrosive effect on crew morale. There is little doubt, too, that depth-bomb attacks, even though non-damaging to the U-boat, are likely to damage the morale of the crew. And even slight damage is enough to spoil a long ocean trip in a craft as peculiar in its habits as the submarine. It may be leaking, it may be unable to withstand the pressure of a deep dive, its steering apparatus may be damaged. In any case, it is not safe.

The table presented above also reflects the great improvement in accuracy of aircraft attacks as the Army Air Forces gained experience in this field that was foreign to its training and traditions. Prisoner of war statements indicate that U-boat crews had little fear of attacks by aircraft at the beginning of the US participation in the war, and the statistics seem to verify this evidence. Out of 51 attacks made by the I Bomber Command prior to 15 October 1942 (eliminating all attacks in which there was doubt as to the presence of a U-boat, three which were inconclusive, or which were not assessed) only 1, or less than 2 per cent, resulted in the known or probable destruction of a submarine, and 13, or over 26 per cent, in damage. In the 10 months following the formation of the AAF Antisubmarine Command, 43 attacks, computed on the same basis, resulted in the destruction, known or probable, of 10 U-boats, or over 23 per cent of those thus evaluated. Fourteen others, or almost 33 per cent, suffered damage to some degree. Thus close to 56 per cent of the validated attacks in this period were either lethal or damaging, as compared to 27 per cent during the period of the I Bomber Command operations.

The mission assigned to the AAF Antisubmarine Command did not mention combat with enemy aircraft, but there is truth in the cynical remark of a young pilot of the 480th Group at Port Lyautey in September 1943. "We are," he said, "not hunting Y-boats any more. We are hunting Focke-Wulf 200's." The crews were instructed to remember their mission and avoid combat with enemy aircraft whenever possible. But frequently such engagements were forced on the American flyers. The consolidated figures for these unsought operations, which follow, include encounters during the entire period, prior to 1 November 1943, during which these units were operational:

	479th A/S Group	480th A/S Group	Total
Number of E/a Encountered	165	55	220
Results to e/a			
Destroyed	3	8	11
Probably destroyed	1	1	2
Damaged	4	6	10
Probably damaged	8	0	8
Total destroyed or Damaged	16 (a)	15 (b)	31
Results to our a/c			
Destroyed	3	4	7
Damaged	7	6	13
Total destroyed or Damaged	10	10	20

(a) All JU-88's.
(b) 5 FW-200's, 2 DO-24's, 1 DO-26 destroyed, 1 JU-88 probably destroyed, 2 FW-200's damaged, 4 JU-88's damaged.

The AAF Antisubmarine Command made a distinct contribution to the antisubmarine effort. It was a contribution that increased in scope as time went on. And it is perfectly obvious that this contribution cannot be measured by the number of submarines sunk or damaged. It is, however, well to observe that it was only a small part of the total contribution by all agencies involved in the antisubmarine war. It must, for example, be placed in relation to the total of 136 submarines known sunk by all agencies during the 8 months from January to August 1943. It must also be remembered that many more submarines would probably have been sunk or damaged by AAF Antisubmarine Command aircraft had the command been allowed to deploy its forces in accordance with its own aggressive policy. Whether such an offensive could have been mounted without correspondingly weakening the defensive patrols in the western Atlantic remains an open question. And it is true that only late in its career did the command receive enough VLR aircraft to make possible any extensive deployment overseas in that vital category. It is probable, however, that throughout its existence, more units were retained in domestic areas than the U-boat situation warranted.

Undoubtedly, at the time of its dissolution, the AAF Antisubmarine Command was rapidly reaching the point where its VLR forces could profitably have been dispatched in large numbers wherever the enemy might make his appearance. Its own plans tended stubbornly in that direction. Almost on the eve of its removal from antisubmarine duty, the command had submitted plans for an extended deployment in Australian, Indian, Mediterranean, and Chinese areas. The following figures illustrate the rapid growth of the power at the command's disposal, expressed in terms of VLR aircraft. Shortly after its activation, the Antisubmarine Command reported 209 operational planes at its disposal. Only 20 of these were B-24's, assigned to the 2 squadrons in England. Of the remainder, 12 were B-17E's, and 125 were medium bombers, B-18's, B-25's, A-29's, and B-34's. The rest were observation planes, O-47's and O-52's. By 27 August 1943 the number of B-24's had risen to 187, the remainder of the 286 operational planes consisting of 12 B-17's, 7 B-34's, and 80 B-25's. It was planned eventually to equip all squadrons with B-24's. It is further worth noting that, of the 286 planes reported in August, 148 were equipped with radar. Thus, although the AAF Antisubmarine Command was responsible for only about 8 per cent of the total aircraft engaged in antisubmarine warfare in the Atlantic by August 1943, the strategical importance of the command's aircraft was relatively much greater than that percentage would indicate. For of the VLR aircraft then in use, approximately 56 per cent were operated by the Army Air Forces, 30 per cent by the RAF, and only 13 per cent by the US Navy, although the latter was rapidly acquiring a large force of B-24's.

In a sense the real strength of the command, as it stood in August 1943, lay in its men and their experiences. A significant proportion of its personnel had 18 months of actual experience in hunting submarines. The combat crews had mastered the complexities of long overwater navigation, of enemy ship identification, of radar operation, of air-sea rescue methods, and, most important of all, the technique of spotting and instantly attacking an inconspicuous, moving, and rapidly disappearing target. They had become expert in a form of bombing vastly different from any other form of air attack.

The conclusion, then, is inescapable that, however its operational history may compare with other agencies, the AAF Antisubmarine Command was, at the time of its dissolution, potentially the most powerful force of very-long-range antisubmarine aviation in existence. To many observers it seemed a pity that its great promise could not have been fulfilled.

11

PROBLEMS OF LOGISTICS, RESEARCH COORDINATION, AND TRAINING

During the course of its operational history, the Antisubmarine Command faced certain problems of organization, training, and material development which were unique, at least insofar as AAF experience was concerned. The command had been invested with a responsibility of a hybrid character, in relation to current military concepts. The resulting problems had to be solved without reference to anybody of experience except, perhaps, that then being established by the British. A great part of the energy and initiative of the command personnel had therefore to be expanded on the solution of these problems. To complicate matters still more, the solutions usually depended on action by higher echelons since they involved the relation of the command to other agencies; in which case the command itself could only point out to higher authority the urgency of the matter, and recommend appropriate action.

The whole problem of logistics, for example, was one which involved liaison with various other organizations and, owing to the peculiar nature of the Antisubmarine Command's mission, the establishment of certain new procedures. Originally all, and to the end of its career most, of the AAFAC

units were stationed in the continental United States, yet they were operating directly against the enemy. Unlike most other domestic units, they
therefore required full equipment immediately. This meant securing a priority rating for supplies. It was not until 13 January 1943 that a priority
rating of A-2a was secured for all squadrons, thus placing them on the same
level as a unit under warning orders for overseas duty. In April 1943, it was
raised to A-1b, which gave antisubmarine squadrons the same status
regarding supply as that of an overseas unit. Beginning in May of the same
year, squadrons were being put under warning orders for supplies in accordance with a definite schedule worked out between the Antisubmarine Command and the Assistant Chief of Air Staff, Operations, Commitments, and
Requirements. Supplies were processed by the use of shortage lists just as if
the units were going overseas. This method proved reasonably successful,
and by August 1943 the domestic squadrons were about 85 per cent
equipped.

The procurement and distribution of ammunition presented certain difficulties. Since the Antisubmarine Command had neither bases nor base
troops assigned to it, but operated from bases under the jurisdiction of
other air forces and commands, it originally became entangled in a complicated system of supply involving coordination and liaison with first Air
Force, Third Air Force, Air Service command and air Transport Command.
Under this system AAFAC ammunition requirements had to be submitted
to these four separate agencies who would incorporate them with their own
requirements, and eventually issue supplies to the AAFAC units. Some
relief was gained by having requirements submitted directly to the Commanding General, AAF, who in turn issued Ammunition Supply Authorities
(ANSA's) to the organizations having jurisdiction over the bases at which
the AAFAC units were stationed. AAF Regulations still authorized only personnel with base jurisdiction to control training ammunition. In February,
this regulation was changed, and the command was allowed to issue
ANSA's and distribute them to its units as required. Supply of combat
ammunition was still not the responsibility of the AAFAC, but remained
with the defense command, air force, or air command which had jurisdiction over the base. In March authority was granted by the Army Air Forces
to maintain certain stock levels of combat ammunition on each base, to be

made immediately available to units of the command whenever needed. Overseas units were supplied by the theater commander except for training ammunition, requirements for which were submitted to the Antisubmarine Command which, in turn, would send the ammunition to the Eastern Defense Command port of embarkation for disposition.

The Antisubmarine Command had, then, to fit itself gradually into a supply plan not originally designed to meet its needs. It involved a constant need for liaison between the AAFAC A-4 section and the service agencies, especially Air Service Command and Air Transport Command. This was especially true before the assignment of a high priority to AAFAC projects, but it continued to be necessary throughout the history of the organization. To facilitate liaison, the Air Service Command released one of its officers to AAFAC headquarters, and the Supply and Logistics subsection, A-4, AAFAC maintained constant contact with the Air Transport Command. The value of those liaison channels appeared especially in connection with the movement of units overseas. As soon as a squadron received orders for foreign duty the Overseas Section, Supply Division, Headquarters, ASC was immediately notified, and special project supplies were usually at the point of destination as soon as the squadron itself. The Air Transport Command set up priorities for shipment of AAFAC personnel and material upon coordination with that command.

Expansion of I Bomber Command and AAFAC activities necessitated extending the system of communications beyond that used in the days when the Bomber Command was asked to begin antisubmarine operations. The usual peace-time communications facilities – teletype and telephone mainly – proved totally inadequate for routing information and instructions to a widely scattered patrol force. Joint action between Army planes and naval units failed frequently as a result of inadequate communication.

By October 1942 the Bomber Command communications network extended from Canada to Mexico along the coastline, between stations from which Army and CAP planes operated. AGL stations had replaced the Navy service, and radar planes were beginning to be used in some numbers. When the Antisubmarine Command was formed, little change was made in this system. The 25th Wing took over the Joint Control Room in New York City. A new switchboard was installed with lines to those serving the 25th

Wing, the 28th Wing, and First Air Force headquarters. With the addition of more signal personnel, the command took on more projects. When it went out of business it had worked out an efficient and rapid means of communication between command headquarters and control rooms, and between control rooms and the aircraft in flight.

Radar equipment presented many problems. Not only was there constantly changing equipment to contend with, but, in a widely extended network, serious problems of congestion arose. When the 25th and 26th Wings were formed in the early days of the command, separate AGL frequencies were assigned to each, which did much to relieve the situation. In order to allow AAFAC planes to move to any part of the world on short notice, they had to be equipped with additional transmitters which covered a wide and of frequencies and allowed the aircraft to establish communications in any area.

Originally air-ground communication had been conducted by the I Bomber Command from a single mobile station on Governor Island. Arrangements subsequently made with the Navy to supplement this system with numerous shore stations proved unsatisfactory. The naval radio stations handled their own traffic first, so that messages from planes were often delayed as much as an hour in reaching the Army controller. A project was begun to install a series of permanent AGL stations to cover the extended areas of Bomber Command operations, and by the time the Antisubmarine Command was created, the Navy was relieved of the task of guarding the AGL frequencies. These stations, operated by the 30th Antisubmarine Communications Squadron, were so located that the direct teletype facilities of the command were available to them, thus providing facilities for the immediate relaying of information between aircraft and controller. As the scope of operations increased, additional installations were made. At the time of the dissolution of the command, a station was under construction at Port Lyautey, North Africa.

Wire remained the major means of point-to-point communication used by the Antisubmarine Command, although a point-to-point radio net was set up in connection with the permanent AGL stations. A network of teletype and telephone lines covered the eastern seaboard from Cuba to Newfoundland and as far west as Texas. This wire network served the tactical needs of the command excellently, at least as they existed in the western Atlantic.

A project for installing an AAFAC direction-finding network, based on general dissatisfaction with existing systems along the Atlantic seaboard, was under consideration when the command was dissolved.

Special cryptographic equipment and systems had to be worked out to insure the speedy transmission of a large volume of highly secret information concerning merchant vessels, friendly submarines, convoys, and naval vessels operating in the American waters. Here again Headquarters, AAF discovered that the mission of the command was unlike that of any other units operating within the continental limits.

It was found, in the fall of 1942, that the existing method of manning the command AGL facilities, by placing men on detached service in various antisubmarine squadrons, was unfair to the highly trained personnel involved. On 15 February 1943 the 30th Antisubmarine Communications Squadron was activated under a new T/O (1-1017), its personnel comprising all those them operating command AGL stations.

The greatest logistical problem with which the command had to contend was that of securing the mobility necessary for effective antisubmarine operations. The entire concept of the organization had been based on the assumption that it should be able to move rapidly and at a moment's notice in order to counter the centrally controlled and rapidly shifting U-boat concentrations. Time and again it had been demonstrated that the submarine situation could change overnight, yet just as frequently the antisubmarine forces proved too cumbersome to react with the required celerity. When the submarine menace shifted from the US Atlantic seaboard, a proportionate number of antisubmarine squadrons was not moved with it. Those units subsequently sent to the Caribbean area, to which the U-boats had withdrawn, found that the situation had already altered by the time they became operational. Likewise in the North Atlantic, it took most of the early months of 1943 to get plane approved for deploying an adequate force in Newfoundland and the units themselves delivered, by which time the crisis had already arrived and was soon over. Only in the eastern Atlantic, in waters the U-boats had to traverse whether they liked it or not, did the AAFAC squadrons find the kind of hunting they wished.

Undoubtedly this slowness in delivering an effective counter-attack retarded the antisubmarine campaign. It also threatened the morale of the AAFAC squadrons whose spirit was normally high. Such units as those sent to Newfoundland were well equipped and trained and possessed of a profound confidence in the importance of their mission. But they found themselves for the most part sharing in the patrol of ocean stretches virtually without enemy, a task which they felt could easily have been done by less highly specialized units. In short, they were not getting submarines. For a few weeks, the 6th and 19th Antisubmarine Squadrons had taken part in a campaign which promised much, and gave considerable, in the way of combat activity. The 4th had been moved to Newfoundland too late even to catch sight of a U-boat. The experience of the 4th Squadron was, in fact, particularly frustrating. An old squadron in the game, it had been organized as an antisubmarine unit early in the war. In the late summer of 1942, it had been ordered to the Caribbean for a short period of operations in areas where the Germans were especially active. Its stay was too brief and its orders too confused to allow it much chance at the enemy. After its abortive Caribbean experience, the squadron flew patrol for a while from Westover field without much action for its pains. After undergoing B-24 transition, it contributed certain units to an emergency project in the Bermuda area where, according to the A-3 of headquarters, 25tgh Antisubmarine Wing, the entire project was about 3 days late, with the result that no contacts or sightings were made. In June the squadron was sent to Newfoundland, but there again the shooting was over before it arrived. Finally, of course, this unit saw action in the Bay of Biscay in late July. Prior to that time, however, its pilots had built up an average of 1000 hours each, with only three contacts among them all to show for their effort. To be sure, they were performing useful preventive patrols during these long hours, but the lack of tangible results could not help but dampen their enthusiasm.

The reasons for this lack of mobility were many, and involve the entire antisubmarine organizational structure. Some resulted from flaws in the organization of lower echelons. During most of their career, the AAF heavy antisubmarine squadrons operated under the old heavy bombardment T/O and T/BA. Each squadron had assigned to it some 50 pieces of transportation, including trailers. They carried with the, wherever they went, field-lighting equipment, decontaminating units, and other implements that ran into tons of cases requiring careful crating and slow hauls by surface vessels up and down the coast. Air transport for those elements of the squadron that could be airborne was usually done by Air Transport Command planes. The Antisubmarine Command had never enough transport aircraft to provide its own transportation; and without that ability it was dependent on coordination with external agencies.

What compromised mobility most fundamentally was the difficulty of operating through devious command channels and by means of liaison between various agencies concerned in the antisubmarine war. T begin with, the command was forced to operate through War Department channels and Navy liaison in such a way that much valuable time was always lost before a movement order could be approved and action undertaken. This was true of the Newfoundland situation, and particularly so of the summer project in the Bay of Biscay. Navy operational control tended also to slow up mobility because it was not originally founded on premises of mobility. Hence the freezing of many squadrons where they could not make the best use of their equipment. This point must not, however, be overstated. Admiral King was as eager as anyone to see that units were moved as rapidly as possible to Newfoundland and to the Biscay area during the later phases of that campaign. The fault lay only partly in a desire to maintain a static defense. It lay also in the inability of all concerned to clear command and liaison channels rapidly enough to permit sudden shifting of the antisubmarine forces. The Germans, under unified command, could move their U-boat fleet with a minimum of delay. The Allies could only follow slowly, impeded by divided control both internationally and, in the case of the United States, within the national military organization.

The officers of the Antisubmarine Command itself saw the problems clearly enough. In the fall of 1942 they had submitted a plan calculated to streamline the Allied antisubmarine organization from the top on down to the individual elements. And, in April of 1943, they drew up a plan to increase the mobility of their own organization. Specifically they proposed that the Commanding General, AAFAC be authorized to issue the necessary orders dispatching air echelons to any base within or without the continental limits of the United States from which hostile submarines might be subject to attack. In order to facilitate the physical transfer of units, they further proposed that bases be surveyed in all likely theaters for possible emergency use; that the command be equipped with its T/BA allotment of transport aircraft to be used for rapid movement of personnel and equipment to operating bases; and that direct communications be authorized between the Commanding General of the AAFAC and other agencies involved in the transfer of antisubmarine units – Army Service Forces, Air Transport Command, The Adjutant General's Department, and the theater commands.

Some steps were taken to remedy the situation. A new T/O was shaped for heavy antisubmarine squadrons, though too late to be of much help to the command. The AAFAC headquarters maintained constant liaison with ATC and ASC. No increase in transport planes allotted to the command was approved, however, since to do so would mean diverting aircraft from the ATC on whose shoulders rested the primary responsibility for rapid transport. On the international level, the Atlantic Convoy Conference defined areas of responsibility for each of the interested countries. And, finally, in assuming control of all US antisubmarine activity the US Navy took a long step toward the necessary unity of command, a step which, of course, eliminated the Antisubmarine Command entirely. The AAFAC went out of business, however, with the problem of mobility still largely unsolved.

Next to hunting submarines, the most important elements of the AAFAC mission were to promote the development of special antisubmarine equipment and tactics and to train personnel in their use. Research in antisubmarine devices and techniques had been made the special responsibility of the Sea-Search Attack Development Unit (SADU), operating at Langley Field under the Commanding General, AAF, through the Director of Technical Services. Several agencies outside the AAF were engaged in the general problems of research in antisubmarine warfare, notably, the Antisubmarine Warfare Operations Research Group (ASWORG), a subcommittee of the national Defense Research Council, and the naval antisubmarine research unit known as the Air Antisubmarine Development Detachment, Atlantic Fleet (AirASDevLant). But the Antisubmarine Command found it necessary to insure, through its Research Coordinator, that the progress of technical development was in accord with the requirements and experience of its own operating units.

Prior to the activation of the Antisubmarine Command, the I Bomber Command had taken little part in promoting technical development. It was a small organization and found its hands full with its operational duties. Furthermore it was still officially a bomber command, and in considering modification of any equipment it had always to remember that tomorrow it might be back on bombardment duty. Some independent action had been taken by SADU and ASWORG, but liaison between them and the I Bomber Command was poor. As a result, a considerable amount of the work of these agencies failed to profit by the experience rapidly being amassed by the I Bomber Command.

When the AAFAC was activated an office was set up in the new organization for the purpose of insuring that research followed lines indicated by experience to be most profitable, and that the needs of the command were translated into technical projects. The A-3 officer, designated as the Research Coordinator, was charged specifically with assembling data on all new developments of any type which, in his opinion, might prove of value. This data he then presented to all command sections concerned, for criticism and suggestion. If the development appeared to have merit, the Research Coordinator requested either the Director of Technical Services, Headquarters, AAF, or the material Command, AAF, to take such action as might be indicated. In most instances, this action consisted of installing certain types of airborne equipment in B-24's, the standard antisubmarine long-range plane, and of specifying desired tests. Occasionally, however, it meant that problems were presented which required the development of brand new devices.

The section eventually consisted of the Coordinator, his assistant, and two civilian scientists, the latter attached from the ASWORG of the National Defense Research Council.

The Research Coordinator attempted to present to higher headquarters the technical problems confronting the command in the order of their importance, which meant that development requests were not confined to devices for the airplane. Action was instituted to demonstrate the need for installing the latest type of radio direction-finding equipment at all AAFAC stations, for installing radar beacons at stations where navigational aids were scarce and for installing Loran equipment at certain specified bases. Emergency rescue kits were also designed by this section and standardized for all antisubmarine aircraft.

Probably the most important function of the Research Coordinator was to keep the attention of higher headquarters fixed on the more important problems. It was not as easy a task as one might at first think, for emphasis was often placed on projects which on the surface appeared plausible, but which in experience had been discarded as impractical. For example, many persons believed that antisubmarine airplanes should carry one or two heavy demolition bombs rather than four to six 325-pound depth charges. After studying this idea, the command discarded it because the bombs did not possess as great a lethal range, a conclusion reached independently by the US navy and the RAF Coastal Command.

The Research Coordinator had no dearth of problems with which to grapple. There were those constant navigational difficulties which were not peculiar to antisubmarine work but which nevertheless were essential to its success. As long as it was possible for an airplane to get off its course, during a long-range operation, especially at night or in bad weather, constant attention had to be given to improving and extending the scope of such navigational aids as the radar beacon and Loran direction-finding equipment. The Research Coordinator advocated installation of adequate radio direction-finding equipment in all operating areas. The command experienced difficulty in obtaining desired results from the system in operation along the Atlantic coast. So it was decided to install an AAFAC direction-finding network reaching from Greenland to the Caribbean. Fifty units of receiving equipment were allocated for use in this special network and surveys began in April 1943. Final installation of the extended system was not made before the termination of the command. Radar beacons were, however, installed where needed in foreign bases.

Radar, in general, was, of course, a major and constant preoccupation of all agencies engaged in the antisubmarine campaign. Throughout the experience of the Antisubmarine Command, effort was made to improve airborne radar equipment and to extend its use. There was no doubt that radar constituted a vital element in the successful pursuit of the command's mis-

sion. By February 1943, radar efficiency had so increased that it was possible for a skilled operator to identify landmarks at 100 miles, buoys at 35 to
40 miles, convoys, small ships, and submarines at even greater distances.
Even the conning tower of a submarine could be detected at from 15 to 30
miles. But it was equally clear that radar had its limitations. It was not perfectly reliable and was difficult to maintain. It required the interest and
cooperation of all concerned, from the command headquarters down to the
individual crew member. Consequently, the training problem was a sizable
one, especially as the command extended its activity overseas. It was difficult also to keep a steady flow of supplies available to radar-equipped units,
a problem complicated still further by the constant changes being made in
the standard devices. Despite these obstacles, it was planned to expand the
use of radar as quickly as possible. Although the SCR-717 A equipment,
considered superior, had never been field-tested it was decided to install it
in all future VLR planes. It proved to be definitely superior in operation and
maintenance to all previous models.

The radio or absolute altimeter, a modification of the radar principle,
answered a pressing tactical as well as a navigational need. In areas of
abnormal barometric pressure, the ordinary sensitive altimeter, reacting to
barometric changes, would give erroneous readings which could be disastrous in blind landing and might easily frustrate an otherwise well-executed,
low-level bombing attack. For it is obvious that, whereas an error of 50 feet
at high altitude would make little difference in the accuracy of the bombing,
at 100 feet it would probably cause the bombardier to miss his target. In a
few instances the errors balanced out, but the odds were great. The AYD
altimeter, accurate to within 10 feet at altitudes of less than 400 feet,
removed much of this uncertainty, and by May 1943 was approved as
standard equipment on all AAFAC planes.

Radar did not wholly solve the problem of submarine detection. A U-
boat sighted by radar at a distance of 25 miles might, especially in the
absence of cloud cover for the attacking plane, be completely submerged
and beyond further possibility of detection by the time the plane reached
the spot. And, by remaining submerged, the submarine was always well
insulated from the air. The magnetic airborne detector (MAD) and the
radio sonic buoy were developed in an attempt to meet this problem of

underwater detection. A plane having sighted a submarine by means of radar might thus conduct an intensive search by using these new devices. Though potentially valuable devices the MAD and the sonic buoy (or sono-buoy) had limited success during the lifetime of the Antisubmarine Command.

Night operations proved to be almost valueless on account of the variety of unidentifiable small craft likely to be met in the course of a patrol flight. Upon locating a surface craft, the pilot had first to fly over it, attempt to identify it, then circle and bomb it if he believed it to be an enemy craft. By the time he had completed these maneuvers, a submarine would have submerged and bombing would have been useless. In an effort to improve night operations, searchlights and rocket flares were developed. These valuable devices were, however, successfully tested just prior to the termination of the AAFAC.

Having located the enemy, the antisubmarine crew faced problems of attack. When the I Bomber Command originally studied the problem of submarine bombing, it was felt that no bombsight was necessary for operations from altitudes of 50 to 100 feet. But tests proved that the average range of error in this sort of dead-reckoning attack amounted to about 175 feet. Furthermore, the standard round-nosed MK-XVII depth bomb was found to be erratic in its underwater travel, and ordnance data, initially received, provided no answer to the problem. Navy and Army ordnance authorities had to be pressed for exact data on depth charges, and every effort was made to develop an adequate low-level bombsight for the peculiar purposes of antisubmarine warfare. Considerable progress was made along these lines. The flat-nosed depth bomb proved much less erratic than the round-nosed type, and several fairly efficient bombsights were in use by the summer of 1943. The latter, though effective, were still in the experimental stage at the termination of the command.

Considerable work was done to develop superior lethal weapons. Among the most promising of these developments was retro bombing. MAD indications reach their height when the plane is directly over the contact. It was, therefore, essential to develop a method of releasing projectiles at this point with a nearly vertical trajectory. It was found that, by means of rockets, bombs could be projected to the rear with a speed approximately equal to the forward speed of the plane, so that the bomb trajectory would be vertical rather than parabolic. This method not only made possible "direct-over" bombing, but eliminated ricochet and erratic underwater travel. The Research Coordinator gave the device a high priority and predicted that it would prove to be "the number one Antisubmarine weapon." Much thought was also expanded on the development of forward-firing rocket projectiles. Though apparently effective, retro bombing and forward-firing rocket projectiles had not progressed beyond the experimental stage before the dissolution of the Antisubmarine Command.

Other projects urged by the command included additional emergency equipment, suitable water markers, long-burning flares, droppable automatic radio homing beacons, and improved airplane camouflage, most of which were completed prior to the demise of the command.

A sudden change in submarine tactics in the late spring of 1943 created a problem the solution to which involved the remodeling of the B-24 antisubmarine airplane. In an effort to escape from the embarrassment of continuous air coverage, the U-boats began to stay on the surface and fight it out with the attacking aircraft. In the face of this situation the standard B-24 showed certain weaknesses, chief being its inability to bring adequate forward fire power to bear on the enemy craft. As a countermeasure, the AAFAC had power-driven turrets installed in the nose. The nose was so designed that during an attack the bombardier and gunner could work simultaneously, the latter equipped with two .50-caliber machine guns. The project was begun in May 1943. By the end of August, 30 modifications had been received. Although in use only a short time before the termination of the command, it was apparent that the front turret had tremendous value and could play an important part in the final defeat of the U-boat.

The projects mentioned in the preceding pages represent only the more important ones in which the Antisubmarine Command was interested. Many others, some promising, some fanciful, came before the Research Coordinator. Of those mentioned, many were developed from specifications established by other organizations, but the AAFAC research section kept constant pressure on the agencies engaged in the work. Actual service testing was usually performed by SADU. Since this group was not under the

AAFAC, but under the Director of Technical Services, AAF, all requests for testing had to go through AAF Headquarters.

The research section attempted also to see that the training of operating and maintenance personnel, and the provision of necessary supply channels paralleled procurement orders. This proved to be a major problem and efforts toward its solution met with little success. The difficulty lay in the organizational structure of AAF Headquarters, where experimental procurement, training, and supply were each the responsibility of a separate directorate. As a result, in the case of two of the most important projects, radar and MAD, the equipment was installed in the aircraft months before trained operating and maintenance personnel or normal supply channels became available.

The Antisubmarine Monthly Intelligence Report declared in its final issue that "perhaps the most lasting contributions of the Antisubmarine Command in the battle against the U-boat are the various tactical and technical improvements, either developed by this organization or stimulated by it and completed by special research agencies."

Be that as it may, the fact remains that most of the special projects undertaken had not been completed, or were not operational, when the AAFAC went out of the picture. It was the opinion of the Research Coordinator himself that the submarines were defeated primarily because they were smothered by quantities of air and surface craft and not because they were hunted out and destroyed with special devices which might have done the job more speedily.

All important AAFAC projects were turned over to the Navy upon termination of the command.

The Antisubmarine Command faced a training problem unparalleled in the history of the Army Air Forces. As in the case of technical development, the I Bomber Command had no preparation for its hastily assumed antisubmarine duty. It had been training for its normal mission of bombardment, and, except for a limited amount of overwater reconnaissance, its units were entirely unacquainted with the tactics and techniques of antisubmarine aviation. Each unit commander had consequently to devise his own methods and give his own men whatever makeshift training he could manage in the operation of inadequate equipment. Only the simplest type of control could be exercised by command headquarters, which was at all times understaffed for the proper execution of its enlarged mission. For this reason, it was several months before proper control could be extended over subordinate units, and still longer before directives formulating uniform tactics and techniques could be published.

It was a chaotic situation that the AAFAC faced after its activation. The first thing to do was to extend control over subordinate units in such a way as to standardize training throughout the command. That would have been a task difficult enough to accomplish if it had not been further complicated by several additional problems. Since the antisubmarine mission was a specialized one, and unique in AAF experience, no provision had been made to provide replacement crews for the command. Training had therefore to be undertaken mainly within the command itself and on its own time, while its units were engaged in operational work. This practice had many bad features, inasmuch as training had often to be interrupted in accordance with operational requirements and as the crews, many of which had already learned improper techniques in actual combat, had to be taught proper methods. In addition, there was a shortage of AAF personnel qualified to give training in antisubmarine warfare. Especially serious was the need for qualified navigators, for that work required a knowledge of navigation unequaled in any other branch of the AAF.

Moreover, the methods and equipment of the Antisubmarine Command were constantly changing. Seven of the squadrons originally assigned to the command were observation units, quite inexperienced in bombardment aviation. All squadrons had sooner or later to be converted from single- or twin-engine aircraft to heavy long-range bombers, and their personnel given adequate transitional training. As the work of research progressed and the experience of the command increased, new equipment and new tactics were constantly being introduced, bringing with them new training problems.

Supply agencies were not organized to give automatic consideration to the requirements of the command for training equipment and material, as they were accustomed to do in the case of the other types of tactical aviation. All AAF agencies gave these requirements consideration when specifically requested, but many of them were not constructed to cope with problems peculiar to antisubmarine operations. Especially serious was the lack of synthetic training devices. As a result of the Atlantic Convoy Conference, the Assistant Chief of Air Staff, Training directed that efforts be made at once to assist the command in procurement of this equipment. Prior to that time none had been received, and it was found that the command was low on the priority list for distribution of training devices. Although action was immediately taken to remedy the situation, by the end of its career only 10 per cent, approximately, of the equipment requested had arrived.

Fortunately, the domestic squadrons were not engaged in operations in close or frequent contact with the enemy. By the time the Antisubmarine Command was activated, the U-boats had practically abandoned the US coastal waters. This was the only bright side of the picture as far as training was concerned, for it gave the command a good opportunity to train the majority of its units while they were engaged only in routine patrol operations, and squadrons could easily be rotated in the Operational Training Unit. In fact, the work of training became the principal mission for the domestic elements of the command. Of the 116,723 hours flown by the command between 1 January and 1 September 1943, 55,324, over 50 per cent, consisted of training operations.

It was with these considerations in mind that the command set about building an integrated training program. Some changes in staff organization had to be made in order to place training in its proper relationship to the other staff offices. The traditional grouping of Plans and Training in one subsection of A-3 proved inadequate. Plans were closely allied with the activities of the Operations Section; and Training, in addition to being dependent upon operational planning, was a full-sized job in itself. Accordingly, Plans and Training were divorced, Plans being transferred to the Operations Section as a separate subsection under the designation of Operational Planning.

Originally it was contemplated to establish a combination operational training unit and replacement training unit which would furnish completely trained combat crews and individual replacements for assignment to units of the command. In this way the command wings would be charged only with that training necessary for the maintenance of proficiency. In this way the units actively engaged in operations would be relieved of all but routine training activities. It was a sensible objective, but one never realized. Initial qualification of individuals continued to be carried on in the wings and squadrons. Such progress as was made toward the attainment of the objective was made after the first 6 months when the Operational Training Unit began to function with rapidly increasing efficiency.

The Operational Training Unit was the pivotal point for the entire training program, despite the many factors which always made a large degree of decentralization necessary. The 18th Antisubmarine Squadron, stationed at Langley Field, was relieved of its operational mission and given the responsibility for all operational training in the command. This was to be a temporary expedient which would be discontinued as soon as AAF Headquarters should authorize a separate training unit. The expedient remained in effect, however, until the command itself was inactivated. The new unit suffered from an inadequate table of organization, still that of a heavy-bombardment squadron. A new one came into being a few days before the inactivation of the command. It also suffered from lack of instructors, especially in navigation, and from a general lack of equipment and facilities.

Originally the OUT course was 4 weeks in length and covered B-24 transition, bombing and gunnery, navigation, and practice patrol. One hundred and two combat crews, each consisting of 10 men, received this course. Later, when increased delivery of B-24 aircraft made an increased number of trained crews necessary, the course was reduced to 3 weeks. One hundred and four crews received the shorter course. It was planned to give each squadron a thorough refresher course, as soon as delivery of B-24's had been completed, in order to compensate for the necessarily inadequate training packed into the few weeks of the original OUT course, and to keep crews abreast of new tactical and technical developments. This plan was never realized, however. Close liaison was, of course, maintained between the OUT and the Research Section. At the completion of the Antisubmarine Command's operations, 20 of the 25 squadrons assigned to it had completed their initial course at the OUT.

Bombing and gunnery training was the largest single problem. When the Antisubmarine Command was activated very little was known, based on practical tests, regarding the technique of antisubmarine bombing. The only available data was that obtained from the British Coastal Command. Subse-

quently the US Navy developed valuable studies on the underwater characteristics of depth bombs, and, when camera installations for photographing
low altitude antisubmarine attacks became available, the command conducted test of its own. But, even with increasingly useful data, training was
still handicapped by lack of antisubmarine bombing ranges. The same was
true of gunnery facilities. Requests for these facilities were approved by
higher headquarters and construction begun on the various projects, but
few of them were completed in time to be of any use to the command. The
result was that training in bombing, technique of attack, and gunnery did
not reach the level considered desirable. Nevertheless, by use of improvised
facilities, considerable training was possible, especially in connection with
the OUT at Langley field, aerial gunnery remaining the weakest element.

The Antisubmarine Command began its operations in the fall of 1942
with a critical shortage of trained navigators. Its patrols made long flights
necessary and pilots, co-pilots, and bombardiers alternated in performing
the navigational duties, using elementary dead-reckoning and radio bear-
ings. Because of this shortage, the policy was to assign one graduate navigator to each squadron to act as a local supervisor and instructor.
Throughout the early months of the command's activity, the navigation
training program was devoted to training of bombardiers and other combat
crew members in dean-reckoning navigation. It was these men, developed
in considerable numbers, who performed most of the navigation on patrols
during the autumn and winter of 1942. In January 1943, graduates of AAF
navigation schools began to be assigned in larger numbers, which greatly
relieved the pressure on the generally inadequately trained personnel who
had been doing emergency duty. The trained navigators, however, tended
to be concentrated in the squadrons destined for overseas service, the result
being that a celestial and dead-reckoning navigation school was set up
under the 25th Wing at Miami which trained 60 officers prior to its dissolution in July 1943.

Training in the operation and maintenance of antisubmarine aircraft presented many difficulties over and above those involved in transition to the
B-24. Even though it was known from the beginning that the B-24 was ultimately to be used throughout the command, the fact that their arrival in
quantity would be delayed made it necessary to attain proficiency in oper-

ating and maintaining the various multi=engine types than in use. In an effort to raise the level of training, three methods were adopted. Some trained maintenance men were secured from the Technical Training Command schools and factory schools for specialized training. And many were simply given on-the-job training. Since training had to be undertaken in such a way that operations would not suffer, It was not possible to send more than a few men to schools for technical training.

By December 1942, it appeared that, for an indefinite period, about half of the strength of the command would consist of B-34's. Accordingly, several officers and men were sent to Lockheed Aircraft Corporation factory, and two B-34 mobile Training Units were obtained from the Technical Training Command. But most of the B-34's were withdrawn from the command just about the time this training program had been completed, and the maintenance personnel had to begin training all over again in B-25's.

Training in the use of radar naturally proved to be a major problem. Highly developed in any type of operation, radar became particularly specialized in antisubmarine warfare. Considerable attention was therefore given to proper radar training at the OUT. A member of the National Defense Research Council was assigned to that unit in June 1943 in order to assist in the development of teaching technique. The big difficulty, of course, was in securing personnel with the right kind of basic training in this line of work. The officers, in general, had received good theoretical background in radar, but were unacquainted with the practical application of radar principles in antisubmarine activity. Operators and mechanics lacked both practical education, and, of course, experience. In addition to these personnel deficiencies, new equipment and techniques continually complicated the problem.

To offset these difficulties, a program was set up in June 1943, with the following objectives. All radar personnel would be procured well in advance of needs and assigned to a specific squadron. Until such time as their own squadrons should be equipped with radar, specialists would be assigned to fully equipped units for training and experience. All radar personnel would accompany their squadron on its periodic visit to the OUT. Mechanics would be split into small groups, each specializing in one particular new development which their organization had not received, and might not receive for some time, yet which they would normally expect to operate. In order to facilitate the assimilation of new equipment, factory-trained Western Electric technicians were obtained to act as consulting engineers, both in training and repair. To the same end, a "permanent" cadre was developed, (May 1943) usually consisting of one supervising officer, two experienced operators, and two experienced mechanics, who were to assist in training of new organizations.

By August 1943, this part of the training program was, like the rest of it, in a fair way to achieving for the first time the results desired.

From the training point of view, the dissolution of the Antisubmarine Command was premature. During the last months of its existence all training directives were completed, synthetic training equipment, ordered shortly after the command's activation, was being delivered, standardized procedures for the first time were being accepted willingly by the combat units, satisfactory aircraft and operational equipment were being received in sufficient quantity to ensure progress, and a suitable operational training organization, based on recently approved tables of organization, was about to be inaugurated. As the officer in charge of training not infelicitously put it, the situation of the command at the end of its existence was comparable to that of a man who, having worked industriously to put his automobile in running order, is then asked to step aside and let a stranger drive off with it.

CONCLUSION

The story told in this study resembles nothing else in the history of the Army Air Forces. The Antisubmarine Command grew out of a combination of necessity and confused jurisdiction. It came into being essentially because no adequate preparation had been made to meet the submarine emergency. Its forerunner, the I Bomber Command, had been asked suddenly to assume responsibility for a kind of patrol activity hitherto jealously guarded by the Navy as one of its own peculiar functions, and one for which the air unit had no special training. It possessed an air striking force and that was immediately thrown into the gap made by the U-boats in the scheme of Western Hemisphere defense. It was to give this extraordinary mission something like precise organization, and in a sense to legalize it as a function of the Army Air Forces, that the command was created. In an effort to fulfill its mission, the Army Air Forces, through its Antisubmarine Command, planned to carry the fight as soon as practicable to the enemy. On both the legal and the strategical ground this command became the center of a controversy which overshadowed in importance its actual operations.

These operations, nevertheless, contributed significantly to the defeat of the U-boat in the Atlantic. It is more than possible that they might have contributed considerable more had they been controlled by AAF agencies. As it was, much of the strength of the command remained tied to areas of defensive patrols, lacking the kind of hunting for which the squadrons were being trained and equipped. Most significant is the fact that at the time of its dissolution the Antisubmarine Command was for the first time nearing a level of experience, equipment, and general efficiency toward which its personnel had been working since the days of the I Bomber Command. Many antisubmarine authorities therefore viewed with regret its withdrawal from the Battle of the Atlantic, especially at a time when the enemy appeared to be on the verge of defeat. It was felt that, regardless of the quality of Navy pilots or the nature of naval strategic doctrine, months would pass before the Navy could hope to build up a force of long-range antisubmarine aircraft as powerful and as experienced as that of the AAF Antisubmarine Command. And the ugly fact persisted that the enemy, though eaten, still possessed large numbers of U-boats in the fall of 1943, and his capabilities for inflicting damage on Allied shipping remained substantial.

Yet it would be romantic to suggest that the decision to eliminate the Antisubmarine Command was an operational decision, or even one arising from the basic controversy concerning the strategic value of antisubmarine air forces. The final deliberations turned not on the record of this command or its potentialities nor on the doctrine of the strategic offensive, toward which the Navy was itself gradually tending, but on the question of jurisdiction over long-range, land-based air striking forces engaged in overwater operations. On this level the controversy came close to testing the raison d'être of the Army Air Forces itself.

On this level of policy, the antisubmarine controversy points to certain lessons of long-term importance. It emphasizes, of course, the need for closely integrated and clearly defined command in joint operations. It also illustrates the essential unity of air power. The chief characteristics of air power are its adaptability and its fluidity. Plans laid on the basis of rigid distinctions of area and function are likely to end in confusion and frustration, a fact proved by the experience of the I Bomber Command during the early months of the war when it found itself handicapped by training which had been carefully restricted to overland operations and inshore patrol. And air power must be employed according to strategic and tactical doctrines shaped to suit its peculiar character rather than borrowed from older military theory. In the light of these conclusions the settlement embodied in the Arnold-McNarney-McCain agreement appears to be a compromise, logically unsound, in which the division of air power into naval and Army branches was artificially perpetuated. Yet it was the only way around a problem which at the moment could not be eliminated, and it contained an element of reason in that it reinvested the Navy with a responsibility, originally and normally naval, namely, the protection of shipping. Yet it undoubtedly left the question of the ultimate control of strategic air power unanswered.

On the level of actual operations, the story of the Antisubmarine Command is less rewarding. Except for the activity of the 479th and 480th Groups in the eastern Atlantic, it is a story of hard work and frustration, in which is told how a great deal of effort and material was expended in an effort to build up a powerful fighting machine which was never allowed to function as its creators meant it to, and which was disassembled just when it was about to become for the first time fully operational. It is a story of much promise and relatively little fulfillment of great but largely unrealized potentialities. In August 1943, AAFAC equipment was nearing completion, the research program was about to provide the command with special weapons and devices which would greatly have enhanced its effectiveness, the training program was on the point of realizing the high plans laid down for it, and the entire organization was on the verge of becoming the mobile, air striking force which General Marshall had hoped to see deployed on a broad, aggressive strategic plan. In this sense the story is a brilliant prelude to anticlimax.

CPSIA information can be obtained at www.ICGtesting.com
Printed in the USA
LVOW11s0323150116

470661LV00006B/710/P